Scotland's Best Churches

Scotland's Best Churches

JOHN R. HUME

Edinburgh University Press

Text © John R. Hume, 2005

Plate 19: Crown Copyright: Royal Commission on the Ancient
and Historical Monuments of Scotland

All other illustrations and plates © John R. Hume, 2005

Edinburgh University Press Ltd
22 George Square, Edinburgh

Typeset in Sabon
by Servis Filmsetting Ltd, Manchester, and
printed and bound in Great Britain by
MPG Books Ltd, Bodmin

A CIP record for this book is available from the British Library

ISBN 0 7486 2178 4 (hardback)
ISBN 0 7486 2179 2 (paperback)

Contents

Preface

Books on English parish churches have been published for many years, and a working knowledge of the development of church architecture has been part of the intellectual stock-in-trade of the well-informed English person. This is a continuing tradition, as shown by the success of Simon Jenkins' *England's Thousand Best Churches*. There is no such tradition in Scotland, where there has been little of the continuity of settlement, of established patterns of accumulation of wealth, and of religious practice which has occurred in many areas south of the border. The agricultural and industrial revolutions in England had a much smaller impact on many parish churches than was the case in Scotland, and there was no English parallel to the convulsive changes that took place in Scotland within the context of presbyterianism from the early eighteenth century, and which found expression in new church building and in the alteration of older churches. Worship in presbyterian churches has historically been a Sunday-only exercise, and for many years it has been difficult to gain access to most such churches. For historical reasons, too, it has been difficult for most Scots of one tradition to feel at all comfortable in entering a church of another denomination. It is true, too, that there has not been a general custom in Scots presbyterian churches to consider that beauty or ornament have any place in a worship space. In the *Buildings of Scotland* series and other architectural guides one often sees the phrase 'preaching box' used to describe a traditional Scots kirk. The same dismissive attitude is often adopted towards the generality of later twentieth-century churches, which often merit only one-line entries, if they are included at all.

This book is not intended to be a parallel to Simon Jenkins' volume, for Jenkins was writing from an established background.

Instead, the present work is designed to illustrate the development of church design in Scotland through looking at specific buildings: it is chronological rather than topographical in its treatment. The concept of 'good examples' underpins the selection of buildings, and many of the churches are in the canon of buildings accepted as being of historic merit. All but two are in regular use for worship. Some attempt has been made to be reasonably geographically representative. But the real test for inclusion has been that in one way or another the church has, for me at least, a strong appeal. The buildings are all ones that have given me pleasure in encountering them, and that embody important aspects of the development of the Church in Scotland – they are buildings I would go out of my way to revisit. The long list from which they were selected had nearly 1,000 churches in it, and it has been very difficult to whittle the number down to produce a book of reasonable length. I have tried to make the individual entries as informative and accessible as possible, without being too architectural-technical for most readers. The concept has been developed in discussion with Vivian Bone of Edinburgh University Press, and I am most grateful to her for encouraging me to choose buildings that really matter to me and to try to define where their appeal to me lies. Ultimately, though, this is not just a selection of 'favourite churches'; rather, it is my choice of buildings which embody thoughtful and deeply-felt responses to changing views of what Christian life and worship are about.

Note: The basic facts about church buildings are not always unambiguously clear. I have tried to steer a way through the secondary sources which I believe to represent a defensible one, but I am aware that the imperfection of the data may affect the validity of the 'facts' which I have quoted, and hence of the conclusions I have drawn. I have, where necessary, relied on judgement based on experience. I am also aware that there is little or no documentary justification for some of my conclusions, especially about the design of seventeenth-century churches. Therefore, I offer my analysis as a working document, not as a finished piece of work.

List of churches by region

Southern Scotland

Dumfries and Galloway
Annan, Old Parish Church (**72**), Crossmichael, Parish Church (**53**), Dalswinton, Barony Church (**139**), Dumfries, Crichton Memorial Church (**150**), Durisdeer, Parish Church (**47**), Gretna, St Ninian's Catholic Church (**165**), Kirkcudbright, St Cuthbert's Parish Church (**115**), Kirkmaiden, Parish Church (**39**), Moffat, St Andrew's Parish Church (**142**), Newton Stewart, Penninghame St John's Parish Church (**119**), Southwick Church (**146**)

Scottish Borders
Channelkirk, Parish Church (**93**), Cranshaws, Parish Church (**151**), plate 21, Ettrick, Parish Church (**99**), Fogo, Parish Church (**58**), Galashiels, Old Parish Church and St Paul's (**140**), Greenlaw, Parish Church (**44**), Hoselaw Chapel (**162**), Innerleithen, Parish Church (**128**), Kelso, St Andrew's Scottish Episcopal Church (**129**), Ladykirk, St Mary's Parish Church (**31**), Lauder, Old Parish Church (**43**), Lyne, Parish Church (**41**), Stobo, Parish Church (**9**)

East Central Scotland

Angus
Brechin, Cathedral and Round Tower, (**1**), plate 1, Gardner Memorial Church (**152**) Cortachy, Parish Church (**103**), Forfar, Lowson Memorial Church (**163**), plate 23, Glamis, St Fergus' Parish Church (**75**), Kirriemuir, St Mary's Scottish Episcopal Church (**154**), Montrose, Old and St Andrew's Parish Church (**73**)

North East Scotland

Aberdeenshire
Arbuthnott, St Ternan's Parish Church (**13**), Bourtie, Parish Church (**82**), Braemar, St Margaret's of Scotland Scottish Episcopal Church (**158**), Echt, Parish Church (**80**), Huntly, St Margaret's Catholic Church (**110**), Peterhead, Old Parish Church (**84**)

Moray
Cullen, Old Kirk (**14**), Dyke, Parish Church (**66**), Elgin, St Giles' Parish Church (**105**), Fochabers, Bellie Parish Church (**78**), Gordon Scottish Episcopal Chapel (**109**), Tynet (Mill of), St Ninian's Catholic Chapel (**57**)

Highlands and Islands

Argyll and Bute
A'Chleit (Kintyre), Killean and Kilchenzie Parish Church (**70**), Achnaba, Ardchattan Parish Church (**112**), Bowmore, Kilarrow Parish Church (**63**), Campbeltown, Highland Parish Church (**79**), Dalmally, Glenorchy Parish Church (**86**), Dunoon, St John's Church (**136**), Glendaruel (Clachan of), Kilmodan Parish Church (**67**), Inveraray, Glenaray and Inveraray Parish Church (**76**), Millport, The Scottish Episcopal Cathedral of the Isles (**122**)

Highland
Ardgay *see* Croick, Cawdor, Parish Church (**36**), Croick, Parish Church (**102**), Dingwall, Free Church (**131**), Dornoch, Cathedral (**15**), Dunnet, Parish Church (**32**), Fort William, Catholic Church of the Immaculate Conception (**170**), Golspie, St Andrew's Parish Church (**50**), Inverness, Old High Kirk (**62**), St Andrew's Scottish Episcopal Church, St Mary's Catholic Church (**114**), Tongue, St Andrew's Parish Church (**45**)

Orkney
Kirkwall, St Magnus' Cathedral (**4**), Lamb Holm, Italian Chapel (**174**)

Shetland
Lunna, Lunnasting Parish Church (**54**), Tingwall, St Magnus Parish Church (**71**)

Western Isles
Garrynamonie, Our Lady of the Sorrows Catholic Church (**179**)

Acknowledgements

This book has, in one way or another, been in the making all my life. My father was a church organist, and as he moved from church to church I experienced a rich variety of buildings and styles of worship. He was ecumenical before the term came into common usage, and as my mother's mother and brother were Episcopalians, I grew up familiar with the Scottish Episcopal Church, as well as with the Church of Scotland. I began studying and photographing churches in the late 1960s, and in the mid-1970s I began seriously to contemplate writing a book on Scottish churches. I therefore started a systematic programme of photographing churches of all denominations, and this programme gained point and impetus when I joined the Ancient Monuments Division of the Scottish Development in 1984, as an Inspector of Ancient Monuments. It then gained yet further impetus when I became an Inspector of Historic Buildings in 1990, and then Chief Inspector of Historic Buildings with Historic Scotland in 1993. One of my responsibilities as Chief Inspector was to act as Assessor to the Historic Buildings Council, advising that body of the merit for awarding grants to all types of historic buildings.

Comparative standards for the judgement of pre-Reformation churches had been set in the 1890s by David MacGibbon and Thomas Ross, and for churches built between 1560 and 1843 by George Hay in the 1950s (see Bibliography). David Walker, my predecessor as Chief Inspector of Historic Buildings, and his team of listing inspectors had begun to look at the enormous mass of Victorian and Edwardian buildings, giving them a respect only sparingly awarded earlier, notably to Alexander 'Greek' Thomson's three churches. The *Buildings of Scotland* series and the Royal Incorporation of Architects in Scotland's regional architectural guides (initiated and encouraged by Charles McKean) have placed much new material about Scottish churches in the public domain. However, comparative standards of assessment for church buildings constructed since 1843 have still to be given substantial authority, and my unpublished work has been largely intended to allow me to give reasonably well-informed views on these buildings, which constitute the vast bulk of church buildings in Scotland. My photographic collection has been assembled primarily with that objective.

In 1994 I was involved, with Christine Milligan, in setting up the Scotland's Churches Scheme, and it has been very good to see that project develop so well, and in a way that encouraged different denominations to find common cause. The late Sir Jamie Stormonth Darling was a key figure in establishing the scheme on a sound basis. From the start the scheme was intended to have an annual handbook, and encouraged by the National Trust for Scotland's members' handbook, it seemed to me that simple line drawings would allow people to identify churches more easily than verbal descriptions. Accordingly, I began to make drawings suitable for reproduction on a small scale. I have continued to do this ever since, and the experience has given me a much better understanding of the design of the exteriors of church buildings. In the more recent past I have been involved with the Church of Scotland (through the General Trustees, the Committee on Artistic Matters, and the New Charge Development Committee) and with the Catholic Archdiocese of Glasgow, and I have had the opportunity to look in greater detail at the interiors of churches and how they work.

This long introduction will serve to introduce specific debts of gratitude: to all the many ministers, priests, pastors and office-bearers who have in one way or another, wittingly or unwittingly, introduced me to their churches; to my colleagues in Historic Scotland, in the General Trustees and the Committee on Artistic Matters, and in the Conservation Working Group of the Archdiocese of Glasgow; to my fellow trustees and the local representatives of the Scotland's Churches Scheme; to the staff of the Royal Commission on the Ancient and Historical Monuments of Scotland, whose work in recording churches is exemplary, and who have assisted in the illustration of this book; to the members of the Royal Fine Art Commission for Scotland between 1993 and 1999, who helped me to develop my standards of architectural judgement; to my family and friends for their support and inspiration over the years, and especially among the latter to John Gerrard, John Shaw-Dunn, David Walker and Andrew Wright.

Church buildings in Scotland – an overview

That there were church buildings in Scotland before the twelfth century is in little doubt. Excavations at Whithorn have revealed the remains of what appears to have been an early wooden church, and there may have been stone churches from which materials have been reused. This book is, however, concerned with church buildings still in use for worship in 2004, so it effectively begins with the twelfth-century Romanesque buildings that remind us of 900 years of recognisably modern patterns of church organisation. The survivors of this first generation of 'modern' churches vary enormously in scale and complexity. The largest and most complete are Kirkwall Cathedral and the nave of Dunfermline Abbey Church, both modelled on Durham Cathedral, and both built with royal patronage – Norwegian in the case of Kirkwall, and Scots in the case of Dunfermline. The parish churches at Dalmeny and Leuchars in the east of Scotland, at Symington in Ayrshire, and at Stobo in the Borders are among the best preserved of a large number of smaller buildings built all over Scotland as the techniques of stone building became more widely diffused, and as the feudal system provided a mechanism for focusing resources on its key buildings: castles and religious buildings. Most of the early churches of which traces survive are fragmentary, either in ruined form, or as parts of much altered and enlarged buildings, though numbers of them seem to have been in use until replacements were built from the late eighteenth century. The early Romanesque style common to all but the simplest of these churches, with its round-headed arches, enriched arch heads, cylindrical columns and cushion capitals, and grotesque heads, has a vigour and humanity which makes it very appealing to people in the twenty-first century.

By the early thirteenth century the round-headed arch was being supplanted by the pointed arch, both for windows and doorways and for the supports of the upper parts of walls. At first, the openings created in this way were tall and thin, producing undivided 'lancet' windows, and closely-spaced arcades, but as the confidence of designers and builders grew, the openings became wider. In the case of windows, the problems of glazing wide spaces led to their subdivision by vertical stone strips – mullions – and eventually to the decorative treatment of the heads of the windows by different patterns of curved stone strips – tracery. Because of the vertical emphasis which pointed openings gave, designers used various visual tricks to emphasise that verticality, such as finishing the surfaces of columns, or the sides of doorways and windows, with clusters of small columns. To reinforce the effect of this, the arches linking the large columns (piers), or at the heads of doors had their faces profiled (moulded) to continue the lines formed by the edges of the small columns up to the head of the arch. These visual devices also reduced the apparent size of the piers, and the thickness of the walls, of the building. Additional verticality was achieved, in large churches, by placing one or two rows of windows above the arches on the ground floor, with the line of the piers carried up between the windows to the top of the wall. In churches with vaulted roofs, these vertical lines often formed the start of ribs which broke up the surface of the vault. In some cases, these ribs were a vital part of the roof, but in others they were purely decorative. In parts of the building where there was no need to have windows, the wall surface was often decorated with raised arched masonry – 'blind' arcading – to achieve an effect comparable with that of a wall pierced with windows. To further reduce the apparent thickness of the upper walls, it was common to set the windows in recesses, with a walkway below each row. Usually the walkway ran through openings in the thickness of the wall, between window recesses, but in the nave of Paisley Abbey the walkway at the top – 'clerestory' – level is bracketed out round the piers between the window recesses.

On the external walls the vertical emphasis was given by the same sequence of windows and by their pointed arches and tracery, but buttresses were also often provided between the vertical rows of windows. These had the functional effect of supporting the walls, and in the case of churches with vaulted roofs, of resisting the sideways thrust of the weight of the vault. Most buttresses were attached to the wall all the way up to its head, but in some later churches most of the buttresses were attached to aisle walls, with a half arch linking them to the main wall-head – so-called 'flying buttresses'.

The characteristic plan form of the Gothic church was the 'Latin cross', with a long arm forming the nave (in the larger churches usually with side aisles, as described above), and a shorter arm on the same axis as the nave, usually unaisled and known in abbey churches as the presbytery, and in other churches as the choir or chancel. Between nave and chancel was the crossing, with arms on either side known as the transepts. Parts of this plan were often left uncompleted, or if completed subsequently decayed, especially after the Reformation when parts of large churches often served as parish churches and there was no particular reason to keep the rest in repair. Above the crossing there was frequently a tower housing one or more bells. Sometimes this was finished with a gabled roof – a 'saddleback' tower – and sometimes with a steeple. In later churches a 'crown' steeple was sometimes fitted. Other churches had the tower on the west end, and some had more than one tower, the additional towers also being on the west end.

This highly simplified description of the generality of Gothic design can stand for buildings constructed with a wide range of detailed treatments over the period from the early thirteenth to the early sixteenth century, and also for some Gothic Revival buildings constructed in the nineteenth and early twentieth centuries. Detailed comments are provided in the descriptions of individual buildings.

Scots Gothic, though open to influences from England and continental Europe, has its own character and peculiarities. Hence the classifications of stylistic variation devised for English Gothic windows do not fit Scotland absolutely. This outline is reasonably accurate and comprehensive:

- Early, with lancet windows, single or in groups.
- Geometric, with larger windows subdivided by mullions, and with simple geometric patterns in the window heads.
- Flamboyant, with complex curved tracery (also known as curvilinear).
- Perpendicular, with thin mullions and cross-members (transoms). Scots Perpendicular of the early modern period does not usually have the flat (four-centred) arched heads of many English examples.
- Geometric, flamboyant and perpendicular windows commonly have cusps – small, pointed projections – to enrich the curved parts of the tracery. In the sixteenth century, and especially after the Reformation, the cusps disappeared, as in continental Lutheran churches. A new form of tracery also appeared, in

which the mullions are extended into the window head a simple intersecting curves – the so-called 'intersecting-arc' tracery.

It should be borne in mind that the building of most larger churches took a long time, and that building fashions often changed during construction. Many churches were also altered after completion, sometimes after collapse or deliberate damage, and the opportunity was then taken to rebuild in a later style. In consequence, windows and other features of more than one period or style are to be expected.

Buildings with Gothic features continued to be built in Scotland long after the Reformation, but distinctively protestant buildings began to be built in the late sixteenth century, though only where the adaptation of parts of pre-Reformation churches did not provide adequate accommodation. There are several late sixteenth-century churches in Scotland, but only one, Burntisland, had a structure that was sufficiently distinctive to survive enlargement and alteration in recognisable form (see entry). This early, experimental period in the development of the presbyterian Reformed church was followed in the seventeenth century by two episodes of episcopal church government, under James VI and Charles I, and under Charles II and James VII. Between these was the Cromwellian Interregnum, when there was considerable religious freedom. During this period relatively few churches were built, and there was little opportunity for any coherent stylistic developments. Two exceptional churches should be mentioned, both of them in Edinburgh, the largest centre of population in Scotland at the time. The first is Greyfriars, and the second the Canongate Kirk. The particularities of these buildings are discussed below. Other churches of the period shared the common characteristic of a Greek (equal-armed) cross plan. A possible reason for this is a connection between the Scots form of episcopalianism and the Danish Lutheranism of James VI's queen, Anne of Denmark, which had become part of her brother Christian IV's system of absolute monarchical rule of the Danish empire. Certainly the plan forms of seventeenth-century buildings for the Church of England are totally different from these Scottish buildings, while there are Danish buildings of precisely that form. Further evidence for the distinctiveness of early seventeenth-century Scots episcopalianism comes in the resentment which Archbishop Spottiswood's experimental church at Dairsie (on a Church of England model) aroused, and in the powerful resistance to the attempted Anglicanisation of the Church of

Scotland by Charles I which resulted in the signing of the National Covenant in 1638, and ultimately to the deposition and beheading of that monarch.

After James VII was ousted in favour of William and Mary in 1689, presbyterianism was restored as the system of church government in Scotland. The form it took was largely influenced by William Carstares, who had been chaplain to William in Holland, and who had left Scotland because of his resistance to Charles II's episcopalianism. Carstares was much influenced by Dutch protestantism, and used this as the model for the revival of presbyterianism, and the reform of worship practice which accompanied it. Importantly for the later development of the Church *in* Scotland, two significant groups, at opposite ends of the religious spectrum, refused to accept the re-formed presbyterian Church of Scotland. The first of these groups was the Covenanters, who had taken the Solemn League and Covenant as the basis of their belief, who had been outlawed since 1660, and who considered that the link between the new Church of Scotland to the state was a betrayal of that covenant. They united as the Cameronians, were forced underground, and eventually became the Reformed Presbyterian Church, which still survives. Their principles, in less extreme form, influenced the development of presbyterianism more widely. The other explicitly dissenting group was those who clung to the episcopal church. They too were forced to meet clandestinely, but emerged in the middle of the eighteenth century as the Episcopal Church in Scotland. As persecuted churches they did not influence the course of church design until the middle of the eighteenth century.

The re-formed Church of Scotland made the focus of worship the preaching of the Word, and though the sacrament of Holy Communion was celebrated, it was done so infrequently, and any hint of 'altar' or of priesthood was eliminated. The emphasis was on the 'shared meal'. This had a profound effect on the design of new church buildings and on the adaptation of existing ones. The pulpit, from which the Word was preached, became the focal point of the worship space, and the audibility of the preacher and the intervisibility between preacher and worshipper was a paramount principle. There was no Communion table as such, the sacrament being shared in a Communion pew below the pulpit and worshippers participating in groups, so that visibility of the pew from the body of the church was not a material consideration. These considerations led to the extensive use of galleries, to bring the worshippers as close as possible to the preacher, and to the adoption of new plan forms, of which the earliest was the T-plan, which indeed was the seating plan of the seventeenth-century Greek-cross churches, the fourth arm of the cross being the Communion aisle. The ruins of the 1651 church of New Cumnock suggest that it was built on a T-plan, and laid out for worship similar to that of the post-1690 Church of Scotland. By the 1730s the pressing need for more accommodation in the larger centres of population, and the availability of large sections of imported timber, led to the introduction of broad rectangular churches with galleries on three sides (horse-shoe galleries). This type of church continued to be built until the early twentieth century.

In the course of the eighteenth century the new Church of Scotland lost its position as the only 'recognised' branch of the Christian church in the country. Apart from the emergence from the shadows of the Reformed Presbyterian and Scottish Episcopal churches, the Church of Scotland itself experienced several break-aways. All were fundamentally about the links between church and state, and especially about the right of the landowners in parishes to appoint the ministers – 'patronage'. Quite apart from any specifi-cally-doctrinal objection to this practice, the middle classes in Scotland were growing in numbers, wealth and power, and resented their exclusion from the decisions about ministerial appointments. There were three major breakaway movements, all of which consid-ered that they represented the true 'Church of Scotland', and two of which retained the presbyterian system. The first and smallest of these movements was the formation of the Glasite church, by John Glas, minister of Tealing, in 1734. The Glasite, or Sandemanian, church was never large, but it lasted until the 1980s, when the Edinburgh congregation disbanded.

The next 'secession' took place in 1738, and though it was slow to gain momentum, proved very successful. It was largely a rural church, providing a focus for resentment of oppressive landlords, as well as a simple, 'pure' form of worship. The strongly-held princi-ples of many of its members led to a series of splits in the original secession, in a bewildering manner too complex to discuss in detail here. Most of the congregations concerned reunited in 1820 as the United Secession Church. The third secession was the formation of the Relief Presbytery in 1761. This was mainly an urban church and was more stable, remaining intact until 1847, when it joined with the United Secession Church to form the United Presbyterian Church. These developments take us beyond the eighteenth century, but define the history of the eighteenth-century secessions, apart from a few remnant congregations.

At this point it should be mentioned that the Reformation did not extinguish the Roman Catholic Church, other than officially. The monks in the monasteries were allowed to stay on until they died, and in some areas of the country the 'Old Faith' persisted. Some landed families remained Catholic, as did many people in north-east Scotland, and in parts of the western Highlands and Islands. In the late eighteenth century, tolerance of religious difference began to be more acceptable, and the clandestine Catholic Church began to emerge from the shadows, starting to train priests and to build churches, as at Tynet (see entry). Official tolerance began in 1793 and church building in other areas followed.

Religious difference was only to a limited extent reflected in the character of church building in the eighteenth and early nineteenth century. Earlier eighteenth-century churches – all presbyterian of one kind or another – were commonly built on long rectangular or T-plans, sometimes with galleries at the ends and in the downstroke of the T. Windows and doorways were usually rectangular and unornamented. Belfries were simple, and mounted on gables. Buildings of this type continued to be built into the nineteenth centuries. The emergence of something more elaborate is marked by the construction of St Andrew's Parish Church, Glasgow from 1738–57. Its design was influenced by that of James Gibbs' St Martin-in-the-Fields, London, but though the Corinthian portico and Gibbs-surrounds to windows are London fashion statements, the steeple is very Scottish, indeed very Glasgow, in style. Gibbs' own St Nicholas West, Aberdeen (1755), though externally more subdued, has even greater sophistication. These U-galleried large burgh churches were the precursors of a whole generation of buildings designed to accommodate the growing urban population, as at Paisley, Greenock, Irvine, Edinburgh and Dundee. Two of these had porticos, and all had classical spires with designs evolved both from Gibbs and from seventeenth-century Scots precursors. This pattern, established by the 1780s, persisted into the 1850s, though with an increasing degree of freedom in detailed design. Similar designs were also adopted for some civic buildings. The use of steeples was not purely decorative. They usually advertised the position of the town clock, and acted as resonators for the bells they contained. Even when churches did not have steeples they often had horse-shoe galleries. A significant number were arranged with the pulpit on the long wall, and broad, shallow U-plan galleries. This type can often be recognised by the pairs of tall windows in the centre of the long side with vertically-paired windows in one or more outer bays.

Some older churches had their walls heightened to provide galleries, the windows being adjusted accordingly. The late eighteenth and early nineteenth centuries also saw some experimentation with plan forms, with circular, oval and octagonal churches being built, but the numbers were small. Another distinctive late eighteenth-century development, based on the availability of imported timber and of cheaper slates, was the use of piended (hipped) and platform roofs. Piended roofs were often used for Secession churches.

In the last decade of the eighteenth century the early Gothic Revival, in which no attempt was made to copy real medieval detailing, spread from England. At first it was the use of pointed arches and timber intersecting-arc, or Y, tracery that were the distinguishing features of the style, which was applied as a decorative treatment to existing building types. In two instances, at Saltoun and St Paul's, Perth, steeples of non-classical type were included in the design, for the first time in Scotland. In 1813 the first of an important new type of church was opened, at Collace, Perthshire. This was basically of the horse-shoe galleried type, with a central pulpit, but had pointed windows, with Perpendicular tracery, pinnacled buttresses and a bell tower, with both pinnacles and buttresses, on one end. The exterior was modelled on a common type of English village church, though the interior was resolutely presbyterian. This variety of building, sometimes referred to as 'Heritors' Gothic' was built in large numbers all over Scotland, often to replace earlier buildings that were too small or too decayed to meet rising expectations. The detailing varied but the concept did not change much during the life of this type, nearly thirty years. Some were T-plan rather than rectangular, some did not have galleries, and some had the tower on one long side.

Another early Gothic Revival building type is what I have termed the 'College Chapel', modelled on the chapels to be found in some of the Oxford and Cambridge colleges. In these the architectural emphasis is primarily on the gable ends, which either stressed tall flanking pinnacles, or a central belfry. This style of building was well suited to buildings on narrow plots in towns. Early examples had the flanking pinnacles, and later ones had central belfries. The type was adopted by the Scottish Episcopal and Roman Catholic churches, and in simplified form by the United Secession Church. Unlike the 'Heritors' Gothic' style, which was dead by 1840, the 'College Chapel' style, though much diluted, persisted until the late nineteenth century.

More or less at the same time as these developments were hap-

pening, a change in worship practice was taking place in the
Church of Scotland which affected the design of buildings. The
infrequent Communions had been celebrated in box pews below
the pulpit, at least in most churches, throughout the eighteenth centuries. The exceptions were those churches in which a separate area
– a Communion aisle – was permanently set aside for the purpose,
in the seventeenth-century manner. The growing number of
Communicants led in the early nineteenth century to the installa-
tion of permanent long tables, lined on both sides with bench seats.
These were either set across the building in front of the pulpit, or
along the worship space on the same axis as the pulpit. A variant
of this practice was the provision of pews which could be folded
out to make a series of tables at the front of the worship space
    In writing about early Gothic Revival styles, changes in the
denominational structure of the church have been skated over, other
than the reintegration of the Secessions. The early nineteenth
century was a period of population growth and reasonable prosperity, and of urbanisation, not so much in the growth of the large
towns and cities as in the expansion of smaller towns, and the movement of the agricultural labour force into villages. This meant that
there were sufficient concentrations of people to justify building
churches for minor denominations. Migration of Highlanders, Irish
and English workers also brought concentrations of Roman
Catholics, Episcopalians (both Scots and Anglican), Baptists and
Methodists into the towns, and a plethora of subdivisions of protestant sects evolved as a direct result of the emergence of large
centres of population. There were also a growing number of
'Independent' churches, where the individual congregation, rather
than the denomination, was the unit. Later these loosely combined
as the Congregational and Evangelical Union churches. Of the very
large number of churches built to accommodate this great denominational variety most have gone or have been adapted to other purposes. The Roman Catholic and Scottish Episcopal churches,
however, began in this period to build buildings of a durable scale
and quality, and in a variety of styles. The United Secession Church
also built a large number of new churches, at first in classical style
(many of them with pilastered fronts, rather than porticos), but by
the late 1830s in Gothic Revival style.
    The Church of Scotland was also profoundly affected by popula-
tion growth. Apart from the replacement of outmoded buildings,
and the building of new churches as 'chapels of ease' in existing parishes, new parishes were carved out of old in the cities. In the

Highlands, where the rural population was growing, Parliamentary assistance was given for the creation of 'Parliamentary Parishes', with a standard range of manses and churches. These were built under the supervision of Thomas Telford, who was developing a system of roads and bridges in the area, but were designed by William Thomson. The style adopted for the churches was a simple Tudor one, with four-centred arched windows and doors, and Y-tracery. The lattice-glazed window frames, including the tracery, were made of cast iron, to a standard pattern.

The end of the 1830s and the beginning of the 1840s was a critical time both for the organisation of the Church of Scotland, and for the design of church buildings. The grumbling discontent with the patronage system of appointing ministers, which had resulted in the eighteenth-century secessions, had re-emerged as an issue, especially as the wealth and power of the non-landowning middle classes increased. This discontent erupted as physical protest in a number of incidents in the late 1830s, polarising opinion within the Church. This culminated at the 1843 General Assembly of the Church of Scotland, when there was a mass walk-out of ministers and elders who immediately proceeded to form the Free Church of Scotland. This bold step – for the ministers had given up their stipends (salaries) and manses – was followed by an extraordinary period when the members of the new church had to build new churches, acquire manses and pay the stipends of the ministers. During the same period the new church also acted successfully to provide famine relief in the western Highlands and Islands when the potato crop was struck by the blight which caused the Irish Famine, in 1847. Most of the new Free churches were very basic, and were replaced or rebuilt later in the nineteenth century.

As far as building design is concerned, two important new ideas emerged in the late 1830s and early 1840s. The first, and more ephemeral, was the first modern Romanesque revival, which introduced detailing of buildings that was directly inspired by twelfth-century Romanesque churches in both Scotland and England. At the time this style was known as Saxon, or British. Though the style was not unappealing, the handling of this style was often unconvincing, and its use often betrayed a fundamental lack of understanding of its roots. Far more important in the longer term was the introduction of a scholarly version of the Gothic Revival. At first this was applied, as with the Romanesque, to buildings of traditional layout, but the impression was much more convincing. The large-scale adoption of scholarly Gothic was, however, delayed by the

Disruption, which seriously affected the membership of the Church of Scotland. The immediate need of the Free Church was, of course, basic accommodation, rather than architectural flourish. Another factor making for a pause in church building may have been the Railway Mania of the later 1840s, which created an enormous demand for stonemasons and other building workers.

Though the building of large churches was resumed in the 1850s, the scale of the revival was limited by economic uncertainty, by the Crimean War and by the failure of the Western Bank in 1857. However, scholarly Gothic became more popular, and in Glasgow Alexander 'Greek' Thomson built all three of his major churches – for United Presbyterian congregations – incorporating Assyrian and Egyptian motifs as well as Greek motifs in his uniquely synthetic designs. His resolutions of the problems of creating appropriate towers and spires, not features of his ancient sources, are particularly striking.

Large Gothic Revival churches were built in considerable numbers for all the major denominations from the 1850s to the 1890s, and were of very variable quality. What one might call 'mainstream' Gothic, largely of French inspiration, was the commonest. Typical features were tall polygonal steeples, with lucarnes, buttressed rectangular plans, often aisled, with horse-shoe galleries, and rarely with separate chancels. Generally the spire was at one corner of a gabled front, but sometimes the spire was in the centre, its base forming a porch, and occasionally the spire was on the side of the building. The fenestration varied widely, with lancets being preferred by the Free Church, and geometric tracery by the other denominations. The best churches in 'mainstream' style are very fine, with the soaring quality one sees in their medieval precursors. Many, however, are poorly detailed, and the use of mechanically-produced components gives them a lifelessness absent from original Gothic.

Intriguing effects were produced by a number of designers who either made their own interpretation of Gothic, or who drew inspiration from unusual originals. Frederick W. Pilkington, and Pirrie and Clyne fall into the former category, and James Sellars and his partner Campbell Douglas, and J. J. Stevenson into the latter. From the late 1880s Scots Gothic provided inspiration for designers such as J. J. Burnet, Hippolyte J. Blanc and William Leiper.

A very distinctive group of Gothic churches was built for the Roman Catholic Church in west central Scotland from the early 1890s to the early 1950s. These were designed to serve growing worshipping communities, by Pugin and Pugin. Most were built of red sandstone, and all are basilican in plan, with choirs treated as apse-ended extensions of the naves. The detailing is idiosyncratic, and at times wilfully so, but the buildings have proved very successful. The churches in Knightswood and Priesthill were the last Gothic Revival churches to be built in Scotland.

The consistent use of the term 'Roman Catholic' is a necessary distinction in writing this section, as both the Episcopalians and sections of the Church of Scotland would describe themselves as part of the 'catholic church'. From the mid-nineteenth century, the influence of the Tractarian movement led the worship, and therefore the design of church buildings, in the Scottish Episcopal Church, to approximate more and more to pre-Reformation patterns. Richly decorated interiors, the use of vestments and incense in elaborate liturgy, the chanting of the psalms, and the use of robed choirs and organs were all inspired by one stream of Church of England thought. Some of these reinventions were adopted in the Church of Scotland, and from the late 1880s they influenced church design, with separate chancels containing the Communion table as the focus of worship, often with flanking choir stalls, and with a wooden screen – reredos – behind it. The pulpit was placed at the junction of chancel and nave, often with a prayer desk opposite. Organs were designed as features from the start, usually set to one side of the chancel. A lectern was usually provided from which to read the bible. The Scottish Ecclesiological Society and the Church Service Society both fostered this approach to church design. Apart from the many churches built for this style of worship, even more were adapted to suit, with the interior layouts of older buildings turned through ninety degrees, and even where no chancel was provided, the Communion table placed in the centre of the end wall, with the pulpit to one side, usually the left. New churches are still being built with this arrangement, though its strict logic is absent from many modern approaches to worship.

Though Gothic was the dominant style from the 1850s to the 1890s, classical churches continued to be built after the era of Alexander Thomson, though not in the same numbers as earlier. In Glasgow, several classical churches were built, culminating in the present Wellington Church, and in Aberdeen classicism remained an active design option into the twentieth century. It was always a style best suited to the larger churches.

The first modern Romanesque revival petered out in the later 1840s, but another revival began in the 1860s, in which the sensitivity of the architects to the character of genuine twelfth-century churches was much greater – the early examples were low buildings with correctly-detailed and spaced openings, and usually with D-plan apses. Where towers and spires were built, they were on an appropriate scale. This modest approach to the Romanesque persisted until the 1930s. The greatest exponents were Peddie and Kinnear and Peter MacGregor Chalmers. Chalmers, as well as building some modest examples, developed it for larger churches, very successfully. His greatest design problem was the treatment of tall towers and spires. One expedient he adopted was the use of an Irish-style round tower, but the best solution was to expand the saddle-backed towers of churches like St Serf's, Dunning. Uniquely, Reginald Fairlie's Our Lady and St Meddan's, Troon is a revival of the sixteenth-century Scots Romanesque revival. Not all Romanesque buildings of the period were derived from twelfth-century Scots or English prototypes. There was a brief vogue for north Italian Lombardic Romanesque, and a few buildings can best be described as Byzantine. Other buildings with round-headed openings have nothing of the early Romanesque about them, and can be identified as Italianate.

The First World War resulted in an almost complete stop to church building. The exceptions are in Eastriggs and Gretna, Dumfriesshire, which were developed for the manufacture of military explosives on an unprecedented scale. There, a total of five new churches were built, one in Byzantine style. When church building resumed in the post-war period, it was confined mainly to new housing areas, and design continued to reflect the pre-war trend to relatively simple buildings, and reinterpretation of the Gothic and Romanesque styles. The largest inter-war building programme was the completion of the choir and tower of Paisley Abbey, and reworkings of medieval churches were undertaken at Bothwell, the Church of the Holy Rude, Stirling, and Fowlis Wester, Perthshire. Of new buildings the most elaborate is the Reid Memorial, Edinburgh. As with other churches of the period, much emphasis was given to the provision of halls and other ancillary accommodation.

In 1929 the Church of Scotland and the United Free Church of Scotland amalgamated, a very important move. Part of the United Free refused to join, and remains a separate church, with a number of small buildings constructed in the 1930s to serve those who 'stayed out'. The expanded Church of Scotland continued to build churches to serve new housing areas, both private and public, some as 'hall churches' with spaces used as halls on weekdays and for worship on Sundays. Many of these were brick-built, a simplified Romanesque being a common choice of style. The Roman Catholic Church built fewer churches in the 1930s, but in the west of Scotland employed Jack Coia of Gillespie, Kidd and Coia to design a series of innovative buildings in Glasgow, Greenock and Rutherglen, the outstanding churches of the period. One of these was not completed until 1941, one of a tiny number of wartime churches. The other distinctive wartime church is the extraordinary Italian Chapel in Orkney.

Even before the Second World War had ended, preparations were being made for a major house-building programme to meet the needs of returning servicemen and women, The provision of churches was an integral part of the planning of this process, but materials were severely rationed, and in some instances hall churches were all that could be constructed. The process of public house building continued throughout the 1950s and 1960s, with large new housing estates built on the outskirts of all the major Scottish cities and towns, allowing the clearance of older working-class housing with substandard facilities. Some of the population of these new estates came from Glasgow, under what were termed 'Overspill Agreements'. In addition to the accretion of new suburbs to existing sizeable settlements, a series of New Towns was built, incorporating existing villages, and in the case of Irvine, a medium-sized town. East Kilbride, Glenrothes and Livingston were the other New Towns. In these towns the new housing was designed from the first to be served by a full range of community facilities, and this included provision of Church of Scotland and Roman Catholic churches. Some of the smaller denominations also built churches. Most of the other new housing areas were also served by new churches. Not since the aftermath of the formation of the Free Church in 1843 had so many churches been built so quickly. At first the new buildings were either very simple, though generally constructed of common brick and rendered, or they were revived versions of earlier styles – Gothic or Scots Vernacular. A key development was the construction of St Paul's Roman Catholic Church in Glenrothes New Town in 1957. Designed by Gillespie, Kidd and Coia, this has an elevated section of roof, glazed on its west side so as to shed light, dramatically, on the altar, The glazing bars are irregularly spaced in a manner reminiscent of a painting by Piet Mondrian. The cross on top of the 'clerestory' is asymmetrically set. This move away from all three of the trends in post-war church design – Gothic Revival survival, vernacular revival and 'industrial shed' – had a powerful effect on church design for the next twenty or more years, when the variety of forms adopted, and the freedom with which they were treated, was unprecedented.

In the late 1970s and 1980s, with the construction of new housing areas slowing down, the rate of church building declined dramatically. With this came a conservatism markedly at odds with the ferment of the preceding twenty years. Square-plan buildings with pyramidal roofs, often with wall-head strip glazing, were economical to build, and were constructed by all the major denominations, either to replace existing buildings or in new private housing estates. It was not really until the 1990s that more imaginative buildings began to appear again. The best of this most recent group of churches are of good quality, both aesthetically and in the accommodation they offer, but so far none of them really, so far as I can judge, stands comparison aesthetically with the best churches from earlier periods. They are, however, more practical as working churches – and more waterproof – than many architecturally-advanced churches of the period 1955–75.

Descriptions of churches

1. Brechin Cathedral and Round Tower

*T*he historical importance of Brechin as a centre of Christian worship is demonstrated convincingly by the scale and architectural quality of the eleventh-century, Irish-style, free-standing round tower. Few structures in Scotland are so evocative of the Celtic strand of the early church in Scotland as the round tower, with its tall, slightly-tapering form, its subtly-sloping, faceted conical stone cap, and most of all its shrine-like arched doorway, with its low-relief carving nicely balanced between intricacy and simplicity. The doorway is well above ground level, for the security of its temporary occupants or contents. The round tower inevitably dominates the complex, but the church itself, built between the thirteenth and fifteenth centuries, is not negligible, with its massive, buttressed tower and short, octagonal steeple giving it a brooding presence in its valley setting. The nave and transepts survived the Reformation as the parish church of the burgh, but were substantially rebuilt in 1806. At that time the transepts were removed and new and wider aisles were constructed, with walls carried up so that a single roof covered both nave and aisles, obscuring the clerestory windows. Fortunately the nave arcades survived this drastic rebuilding. The extension of the south aisle abuts the base of the round tower. The fragments of the choir (which may never have been finished) were unaffected by the 1806 work. In 1900–2 an extensive scheme of repair and restoration was undertaken by John Honeyman of Honeyman, Keppie and Mackintosh, Glasgow. This involved returning the aisles to their pre-1806 condition and completing the choir, which is much smaller than those in most other large, medieval churches. The effect of the Honeyman restoration was to create a scholarly, but *fin de siècle* concept of what a medieval cathedral should be: darkly mysterious, with richly-coloured stained-glass windows. The collection of glass is exceptional, with Morris and Co, Gordon Webster, Douglas Strachan, William Wilson and other distinguished practitioners represented. There is a twelfth-century font. A fine Pictish slab cross from Aldbar has been given a home in the nave, as has a Viking-style sarcophagus cover from the cathedral churchyard. The round tower is in the care of Historic Scotland. Brechin is an ancient market town and was in the nineteenth and twentieth centuries a centre of linen and jute manufacture, and of whisky distilling, the sources of the wealth to pay for the restoration of the cathedral.

2. *St Cuthbert's Parish Church, Dalmeny*

The finest twelfth-century parish church in Scotland, and the most complete, Dalmeny dates from about 1130 and shows evidence of cultural links between the Norse-influenced parts of western Europe. Its sequence of nave, richly-moulded, ribbed, vaulted chancel, and D-plan apse is a plan form also found in Norway, Denmark, northern France and in the Danish-influenced parts of eastern and central England. A north aisle – the Rosebery Aisle – was added in 1671, and remodelled in the early nineteenth century, with rather crude but elaborate Romanesque detailing. It was sensitively restored by the doyen of Scots Romanesque Revival architects, Peter MacGregor Chalmers, who died before the scheme was completed, leaving his former assistant Alfred Greig to add a stripped-Romanesque tower at the west end, on the foundations of what was probably an original one. The south doorway is exceptional, with two orders (rings) of carved decoration in the arched head. Some of the voussoirs are low-relief sculptures, others high-relief masks. Above the arch is a band of blind arcading, with interlaced arches, and above that a section of corbel table, with corbels carved in bird and abstract forms. The corbel table of the rest of the nave was removed when the church was re-roofed in 1766. Much of the original internal detail is comparable with that in the nave of Dunfermline Abbey The churchyard contains several eighteenth-century tombstones of a type peculiar to the western Lothians, and a medieval stone coffin. The building is now the centrepiece of an eighteenth-century planned agricultural village, with no hint of the type of settlement (or great house) it was originally intended to serve. The simple but effective massing of the exterior, and the sophistication of the organisation of the internal spaces are complemented by the intricacy of some of the masonry details, which is subdued to the overall effect. The building as a whole gives an impression of latent power, an expression of belief as well as of baronial aspiration.

3. *St Mungo's Cathedral, Glasgow*

*O*n the site of the first missionary settlement in Glasgow, this great church is really a product of the reorganisation of the institutional church in Scotland in the twelfth century, which created a system of parishes, dioceses and abbeys, partly to counter the secular power of the Scots nobility. What we see today is the product of centuries of building and rebuilding – from 1136 on, but mostly of the twelfth and thirteenth centuries – but it hangs together remarkably well. The building history of the structure is exceptionally complex, and readers are referred to *The Buildings of Scotland: Glasgow* for the most recent authoritative account (see Bibliography). The grandeur of the conception of this great cruciform church, with its massive central tower and steeple, is greatly enhanced by its valley-side setting, necessitating underbuilding at the east end, used to create a dramatic, magnificently-vaulted lower church to house the shrine of St Mungo, its missionary founder. This, and the choir above, were laid out with ambulatories to allow pilgrims to walk round while services were held in the inner spaces. On the south side, an extension to the vestigial south transept is the Blackadder Aisle, at the level of the lower church, a beautiful piece of late fifteenth-century Gothic architecture, with its masonry lime-washed to give it a light and bright appearance. This was the last addition to the building. On the north side of the choir is the Chapter House. The cathedral survived the Reformation with its shell intact but, like other large urban churches, it was subdivided for protestant worship, in this case into three separate parts: choir, nave and lower church, with its fittings stripped out. It was restored in the nineteenth century in several stages, with the loss of its two western towers, and with the addition of a complete suite of stained-glass windows from Munich. Reaction against the mock-medieval gloom created by these led to their replacement after 1945 by lighter glass of which the design has, by and large, not stood the test of time. The choir was laid out in the early twentieth century for 'Scoto-catholic' worship, with richly-carved woodwork. The pew ends display the emblems or armorial bearings of many institutions and individuals associated with the city. Very unusually, the pre-Reformation pulpitum has survived, and now supports the organ and the seats for the choir. The nave is lined on both sides with mural monuments, many of them nineteenth century, and some of them of the highest quality, especially the military ones. The interior spaces are very variable in their current quality. The nave is not a very satisfactory space, very barrack-like in feeling, while the choir furnishings do not complement the splendid, soaring architecture. In both, the visitor or worshipper is recommended to look up as one should in a Gothic church, in order to see the satisfying relationship of openings to solid, and the sophistication of the treatment of mouldings. The best spaces are the Blackadder Aisle and the lower church, with its superb and complex vaulting. Modern furnishings in the shrine of St Mungo in the lower church, while good in themselves, have an equivocal relationship with their setting, reflecting the uneasy juxtaposition of twentieth-century reformed presbyterianism with pre-Reformation Catholicism. Until the late eighteenth century the environs of the cathedral included the baronial Bishop's Palace and the manses of the clergy who served the cathedral, forming a 'cathedral close'. Only one of the manses, Provand's (prebend's) Lordship, survives and is now a museum. The cathedral precinct is now dominated by the gigantic Royal Infirmary on the north, and by Ian Begg's overly-rubbly evocation of the former Bishop's Palace to the west. Between these, however, is a broad band of hard landscaping, in Caithness stone and granite, designed by Page and Park to open up a processional route to the west end of the Cathedral, which it does very successfully. The west end is, however, the anticlimactic end of the building, the product of nineteenth-century restoration. To see the building to advantage, one should go across the valley of the Moledinar (the mill-stream that influenced the site of St Mungo's missionary settlement) to the Necropolis. There, from among the monuments to the rich and powerful of Victorian Glasgow, one can see the majesty of the building with the choir rising above the lower church and the ambulatory, leading the eye to the simple, massive tower and spire, built in the early fifteenth century.

4. St Magnus' Cathedral, Kirkwall, Orkney

*W*hen the church was conceived, as a monument to St Magnus, Orkney was part of Norway, and the church is appropriately in Norman (Norseman) style, modelled on the then recently-built Durham Cathedral, but on a smaller scale. The first part of the building was constructed by Rognvald, nephew of Magnus, joint ruler of Orkney in the early twelfth century, in memory of his uncle. Magnus had been assassinated on the island of Egilsay by his co-ruler Haakon. The first phase of building, from 1137, was supervised by Rognvald's Norwegian father, Kol. During the long period of construction the original design intention survived with relatively little alteration. The west front was constructed in advance of the roof behind it, hence the badly-weathered masonry. The choir was enlarged in a programme of building that ended in about 1250, replacing the original one with its Norse apsidal end. The building was finally completed in about 1540. The church survived the Reformation with roof intact, the only cathedral in Scotland, other than Glasgow, to do so. The building was restored in 1913–30 by George Mackie Watson, who replaced a short pyramidal spire built in the seventeenth century with the present copper-clad, timber broached one. The interior is powerfully dramatic, as the narrowness of the central space and the great drum columns concentrate the eye on the linearity of the space, and emphasise the height. The walls of the nave aisles are decorated with interlacing blind arcading, and are lined with vigorously-carved grave slabs from the churchyard. The church belonged to the town council of Kirkwall, and has since 1975 been owned by Orkney Islands Council. Its setting includes the ruins of the palaces of the bishops and earls of Orkney, and Tankerness House, a sixteenth to seventeenth-century house, now the Orkney Museum. These buildings, including the cathedral, give a clear indication that Orkney was a place of great prosperity and political importance in the medieval and early modern period, when transport by sea was much more significant than land transport, and when Scotland's trading links with the Baltic and Norway were dominant in the country's economy.

5. Dunfermline Abbey

*T*he first church on this site was apparently a palace chapel, which was erected into a Benedictine priory by Queen Margaret soon after her marriage to Malcolm Canmore in the chapel in 1070. It was dedicated to the Holy Trinity and became the burial place of Scottish royalty. The foundations of part of this church survive below the present building, and its layout is marked out on the floor. The original palace chapel had a square nave tower and a rectangular choir, and an apsidal-ended choir was added when the church became a priory. The priory was converted into an abbey in 1124 by David I and the surviving nave was built soon after that, being consecrated in 1150. The choir was rebuilt during the next century, and the bodies of Malcolm Canmore and his newly-canonised queen were transferred to a tomb behind the high altar. The west end of the nave was remodelled in about 1400, when the west towers were given their present form. The spire on the north tower probably dates from the early sixteenth century. The buttresses were added in the 1620s, when the nave was being used as the parish church. The choir was allowed to decay, and the east end collapsed in 1672, and the crossing and tower in 1716. The nave was supplanted as the parish church by the present Dunfermline Abbey Church in 1821 (see below), and responsibility for the nave transferred to the government in 1845. William Stark, of Glasgow, undertook some repair work in 1811, including the rebuilding of the south tower, and in 1904–5 the Wardlaw Vault, a seventeenth-century burial aisle on the south side, was reduced in size under the supervision of W. T. Oldrieve, architect to the Office of Works, revealing the original south door. The nave is the only twelfth-century church in Scotland to rival Kirkwall. As befits a royal foundation, it is on a heroic scale, with massive drum columns, some with chevron decoration. Unlike in Glasgow Cathedral, the western towers survive, flanking Scotland's finest Romanesque doorway. The seventeenth-century buttresses, though they badly disrupt the original design intention, give the exterior of the nave a robust, gritty quality not at all out of keeping with the vigour of the interior. The interior has lost much of the atmosphere of a place of worship, but it remains a singularly compelling space, with that combination of repose and mystery that Romanesque architecture uniquely gives. The ruins of the conventual buildings of the abbey, and of the palace which complemented and then supplanted it, lie on the south side of the nave. Dunfermline was one of the seats of government of the kings of Scotland, probably reflecting an even older tradition. Its role as a royal residence is commemorated in the traditional 'Ballad of Sir Patrick Spens', which begins 'The king sits in Dunfermline toun, drinking the blude red wine', and the palace was modernised as part of the marriage settlement of Anne of Denmark when she married James VI. It was in the palace that she gave birth to Charles I, the last monarch born in Scotland. To the west is Pittencrieff Park, presented to the burgh by its greatest citizen, Andrew Carnegie, and containing the remains of Malcolm Canmore's tower.

6. *Symington Parish Church, South Ayrshire*

*T*he only twelfth-century church in the west of Scotland still in use, Symington's early origins were concealed by alterations until the early twentieth century, when the building was sensitively restored by Peter MacGregor Chalmers. As built in about 1160 it was typical of the Celtic-influenced western church, with a single rectangular worship space as opposed to the three-compartment layout of, for example, Dalmeny (see above). The three-light east window, with its small round-headed windows set in splayed  openings, has parallels in several later Argyll churches, such as Keills, Kilmory Knap, Killean and Dunstaffnage. In the eighteenth century an aisle was added on the north side of the church, with a gallery. The small scale of the building gives its interior an exceptionally intimate and friendly character, and the surviving historic features, which include most of a seventeenth-century timber roof as well as the east end, give a satisfying feeling of continuity of worship. The absence of a separate chancel must have given worship in the early days of the church an inclusive feeling that may well have been part of the character of the western church. The church is on a knoll, like Leuchars (see below), which may have been an earlier worship site. The centre of Symington village dates mainly from the late eighteenth and early nineteenth century, but retains much of the character of a pre-Improvement settlement.

7. Paisley Abbey

Once the greatest abbey in the west of Scotland, and favoured by successive generations of the Scots royal family, Paisley was founded by Walter Fitzalan, High Steward of Scotland in the reign of David I, in 1163. It was a Cluniac house. The only parts of the original abbey church that survive are part of the south wall of the nave, including the processional doorway of about 1290, the three pointed windows to the west of this and the great west doorway on the end of the nave. of early thirteenth-century date. The abbey was virtually destroyed by English forces in 1307, during the Wars of Independence. The whole church was rebuilt during the fifteenth century, but thereafter suffered badly from neglect, both before and after the Reformation. The collapse of the tower on top of the choir in 1553 was not remedied at the time. The nave was adapted as the parish church after 1560, the St Mirin aisle (adjacent to the south side of the choir) was used as a burial chapel, and the rest allowed to decay. In the 1670s part of the conventual buildings were converted into a house for the Abercorn family, owners of the former abbey lands. This house – the Place of Paisley – was for many years used in part as the manse of the Abbey Church, and now forms ancillary accommodation for the congregation. When the New Town of Paisley was built in the later eighteenth century, partly in the grounds of the abbey, materials from the ruined parts of the church were used to build it. The revival of interest in medieval buildings which developed in the nineteenth century led to the beginning of the restoration of the church, a process which took about sixty years under a succession of distinguished architects. The nave and the remains of the transepts were dealt with by James Salmon senior in 1859–62. In the 1890s and early 1900s active rebuilding began under Sir Rowand Anderson, who completed the transepts, the crossing and the lower part of the tower. This phase ended in 1907. In 1912 the completion of the tower and the rebuilding of the choir was started by Peter MacGregor Chalmers, and after his death in 1922 the work was continued by Sir Robert Lorimer and Alfred Lochead. The reconstruction was completed in 1928. The setting was also restored in the early twentieth century, by demolishing buildings constructed within the abbey precinct in a town-centre improvement scheme without parallel in Scotland. Much of the money for the abbey restoration came from the Clark family of threadmakers. The glory of the building as it has come down to us is the nave, which contains fragments of twelfth-century

work, but the 'restoration' of the tower and choir is an exception-
ally-convincing piece of what was really 're-creation' of a vanished
medieval building.

8. *St Athernase's Parish Church, Leuchars*

*A*part from Dalmeny (see above), this is the best-preserved
Romanesque parish church in Scotland, though the nave is a
nineteenth-century replacement, and the belfry a seventeenth-
century addition. On a knoll in the centre of its village, it may have
been built on a much older worship site. It appears to have been
complete by 1185, and is probably roughly contemporary with
Dalmeny Parish Church (see above). It was neglected for many years
after the Reformation, and was used as a barn until its nineteenth-
century revival. The original fabric consists of the vaulted chancel
and apse of a church on a similar plan to Dalmeny. The remarkable
feature of Leuchars is the elaborate decoration of the exterior of
these parts, with interlaced blind arcading on the chancel and a continuous sequence of chevron-decorated arches on the apse. The
corbel course of the chancel is particularly fine. Restoration has
been carried out, but only where essential. Though the nineteenth-
century nave is not notably distinguished, it respects the scale and
detailing of the twelfth-century work, and in no sense dominates it.
This is also true of the seventeenth-century bell tower, the vernacular treatment of which is very much in harmony with the earthiness
of the twelfth-century Romanesque in Scotland. The nave was built
in 1857–8 to designs by John Milne, in a weak Romanesque Revival
style. Initially it was not connected to the twelfth-century building.
The chancel arch was opened up in 1912 by Reginald Fairlie, when
the church was reordered for Scoto-Catholic worship. As altered,
and as originally intended, the eye is drawn immediately to the tall
chancel arch, then to the arch of the apse, and finally to the small
window in the east end. This sequence of spaces, and the view into
the world outside at the far end, is intensely moving, and it is the
construct of an institutional church with a very clear sense of the significance of visual relationships. There are few places in Scotland
where there is a stronger sense of a direct link with one strand of the
Christian worship of nearly a millennium ago. The village of
Leuchars has changed significantly over the years, but the church
and its graveyard, with the enclosing wall, still dominate it.

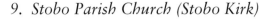

9. Stobo Parish Church (Stobo Kirk)

*L*ike Leuchars, Stobo is on an elevated site, looking out over part of its once very extensive parish. Stobo also bears the marks of evolution of the building over several centuries, but in a more organic way. The original twelfth-century church had a rectangular chancel on the end of a larger nave, and a west tower, like Dalmeny. The twelfth-century south doorway survives inside a fifteenth to sixteenth-century porch, and on the north wall of the nave is another doorway, now a window. In the north wall of the chancel are two narrow, round-headed windows with splayed reveals, probably typical of the original windows throughout the church, and comparable with the east-end windows in Symington, Ayrshire (see above), and in some Argyllshire churches. The lower part of the tower is part of the original church, but above the first floor it was rebuilt in the sixteenth century, with a saddle-back roof, and a round-headed bellcote on the west gable. The sixteenth-century rebuilding was probably post-Reformation, and may well have involved raising the wall-heads, as in the tower. The Y-tracery of the nave windows, and the intersecting-arc tracery of the window in the south of the chancel, are cuspless, a post-Reformation feature. A north chapel was added in the fifteenth to sixteenth century, and contains three graveslabs set in the north wall. There is a set of jougs beside the porch, used to confine offenders by the neck in the eighteenth century. The church-yard contains some good seventeenth and eighteenth-century upright and table tombstones. The parishes of Lyne, Broughton, Drumelzier and Tweedsmuir were carved out of Stobo parish after the Reformation. The area is an upland one, traditionally used for pastoral farming, but the Lyne and Tweed valleys, which pass through the district, have also been for centuries an important route from the west side of the Southern Uplands to the east.

10. Duddingston Parish Church, Edinburgh

*T*his church is, like others of its period, on a knoll, in this case a projection on the south face of Arthur's Seat, the volcanic plug that dominates the Edinburgh skyline. The church overlooks the little Duddingston Loch, and a wide tract of land to the south, including the seventeenth-century Prestonfield House and its policies. The core of the building is a two-compartment, twelfth-century structure, the short rectangular chancel retaining its original corbel table. The south wall of the nave is mainly of twelfth-century date, and its original Romanesque doorway survives, though it is badly weathered. The buttresses on this wall are also original, but they were extended during a seventeenth-century remodelling, during which a western tower was added. The north wing, the Prestonfield Aisle, is dated 1631. Its north windows have loop tracery. The interior was remodelled in 1889 by Sir R. Rowand Anderson in seventeenth-century style, and again in 1968, in simpler form, with the chancel stripped of plaster. The furnishings are mainly of late nineteenth-century date. There are four stained-glass windows in the Prestonfield Aisle, all by Douglas Strachan. At the entrance to the churchyard which surrounds the church is a massive castellated octagonal tower built in 1824 as a combined session house and watch tower, to designs by Robert Brown, at a time when freshly-buried corpses were at risk of being dug up for sale to anatomists. The minister of Duddingston in the early nineteenth century was the Rev. John Thomson, a notable amateur painter. Duddingston Loch is in the background of one of the most famous paintings in the National Galleries of Scotland, the portrait of *The Skating Minister*, the Rev. Robert Walker, by Henry Raeburn. The church is on the edge of Duddingston village, until the twentieth century a distinct community, but now an exclusive commuter suburb of Edinburgh. The building retains the sense of being a village church, evolved over a long period of time and never over-restored, externally at least.

11. *St Blane's Cathedral, Dunblane*

The first Christian settlement in Dunblane is said to have been founded as a Columban monastery in the seventh century by St Blane, who had come over from Bute. The bishopric was re-established in 1150 by David I, and the base of the cathedral tower dates from the church then built. This is attached to the south side of the nave, and built of a different stone from the rest of the building. In 1233 the newly-appointed bishop Clement found the monastery in lay hands and the church roofless. By the time Clement died in 1258 he appears to have re-established the bishopric and rebuilt the church, at least in part. The church as it exists today has an aisled nave, with the base of the twelfth-century tower embedded in the south wall of the south aisle. The tower may have been a square-plan version of the

Irish type of round tower, and originally detached. The top two storeys and the parapet are much later than the lower three storeys, the parapet probably dating from about 1500. The choir is effectively unaisled, but there is an 'aisle' on its north side with a connecting doorway in the north side of the choir. This aisle is, apart from the tower, the oldest part of the building, built in the mid-thirteenth century. It has a vaulted ground floor, and a chamber above which may have been used as a scriptorium. The choir itself was built soon after the aisle, though the upper part of the choir wall and the pinnacles on the south buttresses date from about 1500. The nave is the glory of the building, and was probably built between the construction of the north 'aisle' and of the choir. There is a continuous passage between the clerestory windows and the inner arcade, and the great west window extends this concept, having an inner, unglazed, tracery screen linked to the glazed outer wall by slender masonry ties. Above the three lights of this window is a vesica, a window with its sides formed by the arcs of circles and its top and bottom pointed. The west gable has massive flanking buttresses, the north one containing a spiral staircase giving access to the passage at clerestory level. Below the west window is a richly-moulded arched doorway flanked by more acutely-pointed blind arches. The striking simplicity and power of this gable led to its being copied in several Gothic Revival buildings constructed from the 1870s on. The choir of Dunblane survived the Reformation as the parish church, with some of the choir stalls probably dating from the late fifteenth or early sixteenth century. The walls of the nave remained reasonably intact and the church was restored in the later nineteenth century by Sir R. Rowand Anderson, who adapted the room above the north 'aisle' as an organ chamber. The building is now in the care of Historic Scotland. Dunblane is the only Scottish cathedral to retain a 'close' of houses originally intended for resident clergy. Part of this close is now the ecumenical Scottish Churches House, and other buildings house Bishop Leighton's library and the cathedral museum. Despite massive expansion of suburban-style housing on the southern outskirts from the 1960s, Dunblane retains much of the feel of earlier periods. The impact of the cathedral on its environs has, however, been reduced in recent years by tree growth, which makes it impossible to appreciate fully its dramatic situation high above the Allan Water. The situation, and the west end, are the only really dramatic features of the building. It is, however a building with much subtlety of design, especially in the nave, and the choir stalls are rare and precious survivals, hinting at the richness of the other pre-Reformation furnishings in the building.

12. *Culross Abbey Church (Culross Parish Church)*

*T*his Cistercian abbey was founded in about 1215 by Malcolm, Earl of Fife, and was constructed on a hillside above the Firth of Forth. At first there were both lay brothers and choir monks, but by 1500 only the latter survived. The lay-brothers' nave was therefore demolished, and a western tower built, probably from reclaimed materials, using the existing walls of the rood screen and pulpitum as the base. A north aisle was also added. After the Reformation the conventual buildings were allowed to fall into ruin, and as usual the abbey church was made the parish church, a fairly small, intimate building. It is probable that, as first adapted in 1633, the pulpit was on the west wall, as in St Monans (see below), but the focus of worship is now at the east end. The great glory of the building is the Bruce aisle, added in the seventeenth century, with the monument to Sir George Bruce of Carnock who made a fortune out of coal mining at Culross. At the base of the marble monument are sculptures representing his mourning children. The graveyard to the north of the church has some good eighteenth-century and early nineteenth-century tombstones. To the south, at a lower level, are the ruins of the conventual buildings of the abbey, now in the care of Historic Scotland.

13. *St Ternan's Parish Church, Arbuthnott*

*L*ike Stobo, this is a multi-period church. The building is on an L-plan, with rectangular nave and chancel, the latter dating from the thirteenth century. Adjoining the south side of the chancel is the late fifteenth-century Arbuthnott Aisle, a burial aisle of the Arbuthnotts of that ilk, the local landowners. This aisle is vaulted, and there is a room above the vault. The body of the church was damaged by fire in 1889 and the roof was replaced by an open timber one, with pierced rafters. The architect for the restoration was A. Marshall Mackenzie, Aberdeen. The nave has been considerably altered, but at its west end is a conical-roofed, late fifteenth-century bell tower. The diagonal buttresses flanking the west end are probably contemporary, and have niches for effigies. The three lancets of the east window contain stained-glass figures representing Faith, Hope and Charity. The appeal of this building lies largely in its exterior, which has an almost domestic character all its own. The parish is a very rural one, and the church was obviously built for a scattered community, close to the great house of the Arbuthnott estate.

14. *Cullen Old Kirk (St Mary the Virgin's Parish Church)*

*A*t first sight this appears to be a fairly ordinary eighteenth to nineteenth-century parish church, but closer examination reveals a complex building history. The church was founded in the thirteenth century, but the present multi-period cruciform building is later. The choir, the longest arm of the cross, appears to have been built in the 1540s when the church was converted into a collegiate foundation. It contains the exceptionally-elaborate mural monument of Alexander Ogilvie, who established the college, and his second wife, Elizabeth Gordon. The south St Ann's Aisle was added in 1539, and the church became collegiate in 1543. Great glories are a sacrament house, or aumbry, of a type characteristic of north-east Scotland; the laird's loft of 1602, with pew below, one of the earliest and finest in Scotland; and seventeenth-century box pews. There is also a monument to James the first Earl of Seafield, Chancellor of Scotland at the Union of the Parliaments in 1707. The churchyard contains many fine monuments and tombstones. Like Arbuthnott, the church is close to the landowner's house, Cullen House, now converted into a number of self-contained residences. The present village of Cullen, about three-quarters of a mile away, on the coast, is in two sections: a late eighteenth-century planned village of some distinction, and a seatown, originally inhabited by fisherfolk, with the informal planning typical of such communities in north-east Scotland. The old parish church has outlasted, as a place of worship, a Victorian church built in the planned village. Most of the interest of the building lies in its interior and especially in the Ogilvie Monument, an exceptional example of the influence of the Renaissance on late Scots Gothic, and the remarkable early post-Reformation loft and pew, which between them emphasise the growing role of the laity in church affairs during the sixteenth and early seventeenth centuries. The rather clumsy assembly of external features, with its wide range of window designs, is, however, not without charm.

15. *Dornoch Cathedral*

*T*his is Scotland's miniature cathedral in the little burgh of Dornoch, now largely a holiday resort and retirement village. The church, founded by Bishop Gilbert de Moravia in the thirteenth century, has all the right characteristics of a cathedral – cruciform plan, central steeled tower, vaulted interior – but is about the size of a parish church. The nave was destroyed by fire in 1570, soon after the Reformation, and the choir, crossing and transepts then served as the parish church, being re-roofed in 1616. The tower is supported on early thirteenth-century piers, of Transitional style, and has an early seventeenth-century parapet, probably dating from the 1616 re-roofing. The broached, slated spire dates from the early eighteenth century and was restored in 1835–7, during a major restoration by William Burn, in which the nave was rebuilt, incorporating the surviving west gable. Burn installed plaster rib vaults throughout, and plastered the walls. The wall plastering was removed in 1924, according to the fashion of the time. There is much stained glass, including a window representing St Gilbert, installed in 1989 by Crear McCartney, and also windows by Percy Bacon (in memory of Andrew Carnegie of Skibo, the philanthropist), Morris and Co, and Christopher Whall. The rich Gothic chancel furnishings date from 1911. The church sits in a small graveyard, and is the focal point of the town. Its interior is pleasing and dignified rather than distinguished. The bishop's palace survives as an hotel. It is in the form of a tower house, and was probably originally part of a cathedral close.

16. *St Machar's Cathedral, Old Aberdeen*

*T*he see of Aberdeen was created in 1136 by David I, when he removed the ecclesiastical centre for north-east Scotland from Mortlach. The third bishop rebuilt the primitive church in Old Aberdeen between 1183 and 1199, but in the late thirteenth century Bishop Cheyenne found the twelfth-century building too modest, and started to build anew. In about 1370 another rebuilding was started by Bishop Kinninmond. Two massive piers, now embedded in the east wall of the nave, date from this campaign, and were intended as two of the supports for a central tower. This scheme was never completed, and instead efforts were concentrated on building the nave, the granite walls of which were constructed by Bishop Henry Leighton between 1422 and 1440. It was roofed, and the roof covered in lead, by his successors, and finally the present flat ceiling was completed between 1518 and 1531, at the expense of Bishop Dunbar, to designs by James Winter. The design is unique, ornamented with the heraldic devices of European kings, Pope Leo X, and the Scottish nobility and senior clergy. The design of the masonry can be said to embody aspects of Romanesque revival, the arcades having plain cylindrical piers (though the arches are pointed), and the seven lights of the great west window having round heads, as do the clerestory windows and the outer arch of the twin west doorways. The west end is the high point of the design, with the nave gable flanked by massive towers, with corbelled parapets and generously-proportioned broach spires, possibly the finest medieval, ecclesiastical set-piece in Scotland. The aisle windows on the south side have cuspless intersecting-arc tracery, a late feature. There is a fine porch, apparently intended to have a first-floor room, but this feature was not completed. At the west end of the south aisle is a good Renaissance monument to Bishop Scougal, an Episcopal bishop who died in 1685. At the east end of the nave the arch into the crossing has been blocked up by a wall pierced by three tall, narrow windows, inserted in 1947 by A. G. R. Mackenzie, and the area at the front of this is laid out as a chancel. There are a number of fine stained-glass windows of various periods from the late nineteenth century. The nave was restored during the nineteenth century by John Smith and James Matthews. The timber ceiling was renewed to the original design, and the galleries installed in the late seventeenth century were taken out. The plaster was removed from the walls in the 1920s, in the fashion of the period. This makes the building rather gloomy. While the nave was being built, Bishop Leighton also constructed the north transept in 1424. Part of this survives, and contains his mural monument. Bishop Elphinstone resumed construction of the central tower which was completed in 1511. The south transept was built by Bishop Dunbar, in 1522, and its remains contain his mural tomb. The rebuilding of the choir does not seem to have been completed before the Reformation, and lead was stripped from the building in 1567. The remains of the choir were removed during the Protectorate and, with their support removed, the tower collapsed in 1688, badly damaging the transepts and the east end of the nave. The remains of the transepts, with their mural tombs, are now in the care of Historic Scotland. The cathedral now sits in an extensive graveyard, the main entrance to which is flanked by twin octagonal gate towers designed by John Smith and built in 1832. The exterior of the building is coherent and a convincing piece of architecture. One is not at all conscious of the lack of the choir, transepts and central tower. The interior is unquestionably impressive, with its massive columns and flat ceiling, but the absence of a well-defined chancel and of an adequate east window detracts significantly from the quality of the worship space. Perhaps there may be an opportunity to revisit the design of the east end at some time, or even to look at a more radical reordering.

17. St Mary's Parish Church, Haddington

*O*ne of the great medieval burgh churches of Scotland, and the largest parish church in Scotland. The church was sacked during the Siege of Haddington in 1548, during the 'Rough Wooing'. As at Paisley and Dunkeld, part was retained after the Reformation as a parish church. In this case, as at Paisley, it was the nave that was used, re-roofed for the purpose. The roofless crossing, transepts and choir were re-roofed in the 1970s, by Ian G. Lindsay and Partners, with fibreglass vaults. The squat tower was originally possibly intended to have a crown steeple, like that at St Giles, Edinburgh and King's College Chapel, Aberdeen. The Lauderdale Aisle, off the choir, is the burial place of the Earls of Lauderdale, and contains a splendid monument to Chancellor John Maitland, Lord Thirlestane, who died in 1595, and members of his family. The recent earls have been Roman Catholics, and the aisle, now known as the Chapel of the Three Kings, is used for ecumenical worship. The stained glass includes windows by Sir Edward Burne-Jones and by the modern master Sax Shaw. The organ was installed in 1990, and a peal of eight bells was inserted into the tower in 1999 to ring in the Millennium. The church is on the flood plain of the river Tyne and has a brooding presence, enhanced by its extensive graveyard, with its mature yew trees. Haddington, one of Scotland's finest market towns, was saved by East Lothian Council from insensitive modernisation from the 1960s, under the direction of Frank Tindall, its Director of Planning. He was able to keep the environs of St Mary's largely unspoiled, so that today we can see it substantially as it was when it was built in the fourteenth century.

18. Dunkeld Cathedral

*I*n a splendid woodland setting beside the noble river Tay, Dunkeld is another example of a large medieval church adapted for use as a parish church. In this case the choir, built in 1350, was retained, the nave with its western tower remaining roofless, and used for burials. The choir was refitted in the late nineteenth century, at the expense of Sir Donald Currie, a retired shipping magnate, with elaborate late Scots Gothic woodwork designed by Sir Robert Lorimer. The chapter house, added in 1469, is now a small museum, and contains two fine mural tombs. Behind the woodwork at the east end of the chancel is the chest tomb of the 'Wolf of Badenoch' who burned Elgin Cathedral in 1390. The town of Dunkeld was destroyed in 1690, and partly rebuilt in the eighteenth century. After Thomas Telford's magnificent bridge over the Tay was completed in 1809, a new north-south street was cut across the older street pattern, leaving the cathedral at the end of a cul-de-sac. The houses on the approach to the cathedral had fallen into decay by the 1950s, and were restored by the National Trust for Scotland, as an early example of their 'Little Houses' scheme, to give a fitting route to this relatively modest but unusually calm and settled medieval church.

19. St Monans Parish Church

*I*n one of the most hauntingly beautiful settings in Scotland, beside the sea at the west end of one of the burghs of the East Neuk of Fife, this church is the only part completed of a larger cruciform structure, as the nave was never built. It was constructed in 1362–70 at the expense of David II. In 1471 James III gave the church to the Dominicans. The choir was walled off as a church in 1647, and the transepts abandoned. In 1826–8 William Burn re-roofed the transepts and re-created the pre-Reformation space, with plaster ceiling and mouldings. The building was repaired and re-roofed by Peter MacGregor Chalmers in 1899, who also rebuilt the parapet of the tower The building was again restored in 1955 by Ian G. Lindsay and Partners, who stripped out Burn's plasterwork and replaced his vaults over the crossing and transepts by timber panelling. The lime-washing dates from this period. The choir is elaborately vaulted, with heraldic bosses. The church is now arranged as a conventional T-plan, with the pulpit on the north wall of the crossing, the furnishings dating from 1955–61. The pre-Reformation use of the church is recalled by the survival of a fine set of sedilia and a credence in the choir, and of sacrament houses and a piscina in the transepts. Model ships are suspended from the vaults in the transepts, as St Monans was for many years a fishing and boat-building community. There is something immensely satisfying about this little church, with its short steepled tower and buttressed walls, within sound of the sea, the epitome of the place of worship in medieval Fife, despite its much longer use as a presbyterian church.

20. *Holy Trinity Parish Church, St Andrews*

*P*eter MacGregor Chalmers, architect of the extensive rebuilding of this church, was a man who immersed himself in the architecture of medieval Scotland to the extent that it is sometimes difficult to know where original work ends and Chalmers' work begins. Nowhere is this more evident than at Holy Trinity, where what appears to be an authentic fifteenth-century building is almost all MacGregor Chalmers, and very fine too. Only the tower and some of the columns are fifteenth-century work, begun in 1411. The spire dates from the sixteenth century. The body of the medieval church had been rebuilt in 1798–1899, and again altered in 1863, so that Chalmers was faced with recovering the medieval fragments which had survived this work. Of the other original fabric, the most interesting is the black and white marble mural monument to Archbishop Sharp, who was assassinated in 1679. This shows the archbishop kneeling, with an angel hovering over his head. The figure is set in an elaborately-detailed, Renaissance classical architrave. There are also two sixteenth-century oak choir stalls, a rare survival. The interior is set out for Scoto-catholic worship. The stained glass all dates from the MacGregor Chalmers period, and includes work by Douglas Strachan. The building, also known as the Town Kirk, is in the heart of the burgh, in a little square, and surrounded on three sides by buildings of a complementary scale. The interior has the clarity of organisation of space that characterises all MacGregor Chalmers's work, and faithfully evokes the spirit of the late Gothic in Scotland.

21. St Michael's Parish Church, Linlithgow

*I*n some respects this is a typical burgh church, but though physically it is similar to others – cruciform, with aisled nave and choir – it is unusual in its juxtaposition with the royal palace of Linlithgow, with which it had a close relationship, though there was also a chapel in the south range of the palace. There was an earlier building on this site, but the church that still exists was rebuilt from the 1420s, starting with the nave and tower, which was originally topped by a crown steeple. The choir dates from 1489–1532, and has a semi-octagonal apsidal end, with cuspless, Perpendicular tracery in the windows, both fashionable in about 1500. The apse was walled off during a 'restoration' of 1812, in which the crown steeple was removed. The building was then taken in hand in 1894–6 by John Honeyman and John Keppie, of Glasgow, and the galleries and box pews installed in 1812 and later were cleared away. In 1964, after proposals to reinstate the crown steeple were rejected, an aluminium-covered timber steeple was put up in its place. This was startling in its day, but is now a well-accepted local landmark. There are some fine stained-glass windows in the building, the most recent one, in the south transept, being by Crear McCartney. The flamboyant tracery of this extraordinary window, the upper part of which has three curved sides of equal length, provides a splendid setting for what is, in my view, one of the finest modern windows in Scotland. Though Linlithgow has expanded markedly in the late twentieth century, its centre retains its medieval plan, with its winding main street lined with burgage plots, widening out in the centre to form a market place. The processional route from the market place to the palace and parish church retains much of its sixteenth to seventeenth-century character.

22. St John's Parish Church, Perth

*P*erth, at the head of the Tay navigation, and on the principal routes between northern and southern Scotland, was one of the most important Scottish burghs before the Reformation. Its burgh church is on an appropriate scale and, as at Holy Trinity, St Andrews, is set in a town square, in the heart of the 'Fair City'. It was built from about 1440 to replace a twelfth-century building. The choir was the first part to be constructed, followed by the transepts and tower, and finally the nave and the Halkerston Tower, which functions as the north porch. The leadwork of the timber broach spire dates from the mid-eighteenth century. As in the case of most other large medieval churches, the building was subdivided after the Reformation, but was restored in the 1820s by James Gillespie Graham, and again in the 1890s by Andrew Heiton junior In 1923–6 Sir Robert Lorimer made further alterations, including heightening the aisles, and installing new woodwork, made by Scott Morton of Edinburgh. The choir roof is original fifteenth-century work. There is a fine collection of stained glass, by William Wilson, Meikle and Son, Douglas Strachan, Stephen Adam and Louis Davis. Close up, the dun-coloured local stone detracts from the impact of what is an attractive building. Its most distinctive feature is the lead-covered broach spire over the crossing, a landmark of which glimpses can be seen from many parts of the city. Because of the restricted site it is difficult to appreciate the church as a whole.

23. Fowlis Easter Parish Church

*H*idden away in what is still countryside to the west of the city of Dundee, this externally modest church, with its generally simple, late Gothic detailing, contains some remarkable original features. It is on a long rectangular plan, and appears to have been built in the middle of the fifteenth century for Sir Andrew Gray of Fowlis and Aberdour. The corbels for a rood screen and loft survive, as does one of the doors of the screen, with two flamboyant low-relief panels of tracery, and three full and two engaged uprights above, all delicately crocketted. There is an ornate sacrament house, or aumbry, with a bust of Christ in majesty, flanked by full figures of angels. On a cornice above are figures representing the Annunciation. The base of an elaborate font, and a holy water stoup, also survive. As if this were not sufficiently remarkable, there are four religious paintings from before the Reformation, which are hung on the east and south walls. The nave was partitioned off as the parish church after the Reformation, but the two parts were reunited in the late nineteenth century by T. S. Robertson, who put a new, open timber roof on the building. The survival of so much pre-Reformation material is evidence of a continuing respect and sympathy for the 'Old Religion' at a time when such an attitude was politically dangerous.

24. *St Matthew's Scottish Episcopal Chapel, Roslin (Rosslyn Chapel)*

*W*ell known, almost notorious, for its architectural elaboration and supposed secrets, Rosslyn could not be omitted from this volume. It was built for William Sinclair, third Earl of Orkney from 1450, and was never finished – what we see is the choir of a church which would have been almost cathedral-like in scale. It was probably originally intended to have a timber roof (or a stone-slab one) over its vault. The exposed vault has proved less than waterproof, threatening damage to the elaborate decoration within, on virtually every surface. It has been described as 'wedding-cake' decoration, but I see it as more like Christmas cake – rich to the point of indigestibility. It is worth seeing simply as an example of decoration run riot, a marked contrast to the relative simplicity of most Scots Gothic. It has been suggested that the decoration is inspired by the Manueline architecture of Spain and Portugal, but the chronology is wrong. As I write, the building is still protected by a temporary roof, installed to allow the vault to dry out, pending a long-term conservation solution.

25. *Kilbirnie Old Parish Church (Kilbirnie Auld Kirk)*

*I*f Rosslyn represents a high point in pre-Reformation elaboration, Kilbirnie Auld Kirk is, internally, an exceptional example of elaborate Reformed craftsmanship. It was built in 1470 as a parish church for a small burgh, as an unaisled building with a tower at the west end, added in 1490. After the Reformation aisles were added for the Crawfords of Glengarnock (1597) and for the Crawford family (1642). Finally a transept and a new entrance front, on the north side of the building, were added in 1903–5, designed by S. S. Johnston. The interior is, as a result of this building history, visually bewildering, and filled with pews in a complex layout. The dominant feature is the Renaissance Crawford loft, built for the first Viscount Garnock in about 1705, incomparably the most remarkable piece of early eighteenth-century woodwork in a Scottish church. This has

Corinthian columns supporting the front of a bowed canopy, Both the canopy and the gallery front are embellished with armorial panels relating to the lineage of the family. In comparison, the pulpit and Ladyland loft, both of seventeenth to eighteenth-century date, which would be striking in any other setting, seem almost insignificant. If the building lacks architectural coherence, both internally and externally, this does not detract from its compelling atmosphere. Nowhere else in Scotland is there a more palpable sense of the continuity of worship since the fifteenth century and of succeeding generations' tolerance of their predecessors' vision of what a worship space should be. It is all the more surprising that this should be the case, as Kilbirnie and Glengarnock were heavily industrialised from the early nineteenth century until the late twentieth century. The graveyard behind the church contains the Crawford tomb of 1592, with similar detailing to the near-contemporary Crawford of Glengarnock aisle, which contains the recumbent effigies of Thomas Crawford of Jordanhill and his wife Janet Ker of Kersland. The historic core of the burgh of Kilbirnie lies to the west of the church.

26. Corstorphine Old Parish Church, Edinburgh

Corstorphine was until the late nineteenth century a small village on the outskirts of Edinburgh. It became a dormitory suburb after the opening of a branch railway, and in the 1920s was embedded within the built-up area of the city with the construction of a large number of bungalows, and of an electric tramway. Corstorphine Old Church is in the centre of what remains of the old village. Apparently a simple village church, it has a more complex building history than that. It was founded as a private collegiate church by Sir Adam Forrester in 1405, on a site to the south of the parish church. The nave was the first part built, and was followed, probably in the 1440s, by the choir and west tower. The medieval parish church was demolished in 1646, and a north aisle was built on to the collegiate church, which became the parish church. The 1646 aisle was replaced in 1828 to designs by William Burn. A major overhaul of the structure was undertaken in 1903–5 by George Henderson, with the roof of the nave being replaced by a vault made of concrete (granolithic) slabs, covered with slabs of the same material, to resemble the stone-slab roof of the chancel. The galleries were removed at the same time. In the interior are good

mural tombs to members of the Forrester family. The worship space is laid out in the Scoto-catholic manner.

27. *The Steeple and Town Churches, Dundee*

*I*n the cities of Aberdeen, Edinburgh, Glasgow and Dundee the large burgh churches (and in Glasgow's case the cathedral) were subdivided after the Reformation to serve more than one congregation. In Dundee alone this phenomenon has persisted, even though most of the original fabric has gone. The steeple, more properly a saddle-back tower (a characteristic Scots feature), is all that obviously survives from the medieval church. And what a survival, for this is the grandest tower of its period in Scotland, of a massive simplicity in design. It was built in about 1460, on the east end of the cruciform burgh church. The nave was burned out during the English wars of the 1540s, and not immediately repaired. As usual with large medieval churches, the rest of the building was subdivided after the Reformation, in this case into three churches. To cope with the growing population of the burgh, the nave was rebuilt in 1787–8 to designs by Samuel Bell, in a simple 'Gothick' style, and it is known as the Steeple Church. The three churches in the choir, crossing and transepts were destroyed in a spectacular fire in 1841, and rebuilt in 1842–7 as a single church – St Mary's – to designs by William Burn. Burn's work is an early example of scholarly Gothic Revival. Since the 1960s the complex has been enclosed on the north and west sides by a shopping centre. This shopping centre was itself rebuilt in the 1990s and the layout was adjusted to enable the tower to be seen to advantage. This remarkable structure therefore still dominates central Dundee, as it was originally designed to do.

28. *The High Church of St Giles (St Giles' Cathedral), Edinburgh*

*T*his church is in the heart of the Old Town of Edinburgh, and was founded in the twelfth century as the burgh church. A twelfth-century doorway on the north side of the nave survived until 1796. St Giles was rebuilt in stages in the fourteenth, fifteenth and sixteenth centuries. It was originally built as a cruciform church, but the present plan is of unusual complexity, as chapels and aisles were added in a manner very unusual in Scotland. The first section consisted of four of the bays of the choir, the crossing, the lower part of the tower, the inner bays of the transepts, and the whole of the nave. In the mid-fifteenth century the two eastern bays of the choir were rebuilt, a clerestory was added, and the tower was heightened. The crown steeple, a symbol of the imperial aspirations of the Scottish monarchy, was added in the late 1490s. Even before the rebuilding of the body of the church had started, the addition of 'aisles' had begun in the 1390s, and this continued until 1518. The post-Reformation history of the building is unusually complex. As usual with large churches, it was subdivided, in this case into three, but when it was designated a cathedral in 1633 it was reunited. In 1639, however, the divisions were restored. At different times in the succeeding years, parts of the building were used as a meeting place for the Scottish Parliament, as an extension of the Tolbooth (which stood next to the church), as accommodation for the General Assembly of the Church of Scotland, and as part of the Supreme Courts of Scotland. With building land at a premium in the burgh, shops – luckenbooths – were built against the walls of the church, and remained there until the early nineteenth century, when they, and the Tolbooth, were cleared away and the frontage of the Supreme Courts was rebuilt. At that time the building contained four churches, a hall for the General Assembly, police offices and a fire-engine house. Clearance of the surrounding buildings revealed that the exterior of the church was in poor condition. In consequence a fairly drastic 'restoration' was undertaken by William Burn between 1829 and 1833. Burn completely recased the body of the church, with only the superb crown steeple escaping this fate. He remodelled the interior to form three separate churches. Further restoration took place in the 1870s and 1880s, to create a single worship space. The choir came first (1871–3), then the south transept and Preston Aisle (1878–9), and finally, in 1881–3, the nave, crossing and north transept. The last phase included the remodelling of the west front in an elaborate but clumsy manner. The most recent large-scale intervention was the building of the Thistle Chapel adjacent to the north-east corner of the church. Designed by Sir Robert Lorimer, this very tall, narrow space is decorated with a richness only paralleled in Rosslyn Chapel. Here it works better, for there is a coherence in it that is lacking in Rosslyn. It is essentially a functional space, a chapel for the knights and ladies of the Order of the Thistle, designed to give them the dignity due to members of this very select order of chivalry, and that it does, magnificently. The interior of the main body of the church, though suitably Gothic and mysterious, lacks coherence because of the complex plan, the various effect being enhanced by an eclectic set of mural monuments, mostly Victorian and later. Some of these are of exceptional quality. In the late twentieth century attempts have been made to create a more effective focus for worship at the crossing, As part of this refocusing, a large new organ, given by the Salvesen family, has been installed in the south transept, and pews have been replaced by seats. The general effect is fascinating, but not entirely convincing. The crown steeple, however, continues to float above this visual confusion, a serene reminder of the imperial aspirations of the later Stewart monarchs, but more particularly of Edinburgh's status as the capital city of Scotland.

29. *The Church of the Holy Rude, Stirling*

*T*he last example of a great medieval burgh church in this book, the Holy Rude was built between 1456 and the early sixteenth century. The nave and the lower part of the western tower were built between 1466 and 1470, presumably on to an earlier choir. The church retains its original open timber roof, and has vaulted aisles. The design incorporated provision for a central tower, in the shape of the massive piers at the crossing. The choir was rebuilt from 1507, at the same time as the western tower was completed. The east end was treated as a semi-octagonal apse, as was fashionable at the time. Because the site is sloping, this is underbuilt, giving the heavily-buttressed exterior a dramatic effect. The apse is vaulted, and has a stone-slab roof, another feature fashionable in the early sixteenth century. Like many other large churches, the Holy Rude was divided after the Reformation, in this case into two. They were reunited, in 1936, by the Stirling-born architect James Miller, who added a new south transept to the choir and nave. It is virtually impossible to view the church as whole, but the choir, with its apsidal end, is the most striking thing of its kind in Scotland, a fitting landmark on the long climb up Spittal Street to Stirling's great castle and royal palace. The choir was the scene of the christening of James VI in 1566, for the church was used by royalty when they were in residence in Stirling until the building of the Chapel Royal in Stirling Castle in 1594. The nave, though less striking externally, is a dignified space internally, still with its original timber roof trusses, which were obscured by a plaster ceiling for many years, until the 1936 restoration. At the west end is the tower. Although the impact of the tower is diminished by the rising ground of the churchyard to the west, it is extraordinarily dignified in its proportions and simple detailing. To the south side of the church is Cowane's Hospital, or the Guildhall, with its contemporary bowling green, a potent symbol of the post-Reformation Scots burgh. This contrasts with the northern neighbour of the church, Mar's Wark, an elaborate Renaissance palace built to demonstrate the wealth and taste of a courtier – but economically so with a row of shops on its ground floor! These buildings, the large burgh houses, some mid-twentieth-century, vernacular revival, public housing, and the Scots renaissance Argyll's Lodging form an architectural and historical ensemble of unique interest and charm.

30. King's College Chapel, Old Aberdeen

*C*lear evidence for the wealth, taste and ambitions of King's College, the first part of the University of Aberdeen, this chapel dates from about 1500. With its crown steeple, it hovers conceptually between the medieval and the high Renaissance. The west show front has the steeple at its south-west corner, and the west window is round-headed, an example of the Romanesque revival of the period (like the west front of St Machar's Cathedral, a short distance to the north) though the tracery within it is of the curvilinear pattern characteristic of late Scots Gothic. Internally, the chapel has the finest surviving pre-Reformation woodwork in Scotland: a screen and set of choir stalls. The steeple blew down in 1633, and was rebuilt with a grant from Charles I. The chapel is the focal point of the College as it developed from the early sixteenth century, with the old library to the east and twentieth-century buildings to the north, Opposite it are some of the buildings of Old Aberdeen, now an enclave in the vast campus of the modern University of Aberdeen, which abandoned its other college – Marischal – in the city centre in favour of expansion on the flatter, and less-valuable, land round King's College.

31. St Mary's Parish Church, Ladykirk

*D*efiantly situated at the top of the valley of the river Tweed, looking over to Norham in England, Ladykirk is the most complete and least altered of the stone-slab roofed churches which were built in eastern Scotland in the early sixteenth century. It was built in about 1500 and is cruciform in plan, with a tower at the west end and a semi-octagonal east end, typical of the period. Unusually, the transepts also have semi-octagonal ends. Internally it has pointed barrel vaults. The domical-roofed belfry stage of the tower was added in 1743, possibly to a design by William Adam. At some time after the Reformation, possibly in 1743, the west end of the church was turned into a schoolroom. The division was removed and the building repaired in 1861. It was probably at that time that a central pulpit was fitted into the apse at the east end, giving a rather odd effect. There are some chaste marble memorial tablets on the walls.

32. Dunnet Parish Church

*T*his is often used as an example of the plain, unadorned Scots kirk, but the validity of this view is open to question. The harled walls of the body of the church, which may date from the sixteenth century, may well conceal what has been a rather different building. The tower, which is now its dominant and distinctive feature, was added in about 1700. A north aisle was added in 1836–7, when the present box pews were installed. In the entrance there is a memorial to the Rev. Timothy Pont, minister of Dunnet from 1601 to 1610, but better known for his pioneering mapping of large parts of Scotland. In its present form the building has a solid, rather chunky charm, a sense of growing out of its churchyard. The deep-set rectangular windows and the saddle-back bell tower reinforce the vigour of the design, showing how the sense of proportion of its successive builders made them create a structure with a sculptural quality which could hardly be matched by a twentieth-century minimalist architect. Small wonder that mid-twentieth-century architects, seeking inspiration for simple modern churches of Scots character, chose this one as a model, though they never achieved the sense of inevitability of Dunnet.

33. *Burntisland Parish Church*

One of the most remarkable churches of any generation in Scotland, and eventually an influence on mid-twentieth-century church design, Burntisland was one of the first churches in Scotland built after the Reformation. It was constructed by the town council, using the proceeds of a tax on timber imported through Burntisland Harbour. The body of the church was built between 1592 and 1596, and its original timber steeple was added in 1600. The building is square in plan, with an internal square formed by four arches supporting a central bell tower. At the corners of the internal square, diagonal arches link the central columns to the corners of the building, which are buttressed to resist the thrust of these arches. The walls and steeple were originally lower than they are now. The steeple was rebuilt in stone in 1748, retaining the original weathercock of 1600, and the walls were raised in 1822. Originally there were no galleries. These were inserted between c. 1602 and 1630, and the gallery fronts have painted decoration. The Seamen's Loft has its own external stair, installed in 1679. The most remarkable internal feature is the so-called Magistrates' Pew, fitted round one of the columns. This was installed in 1606 as the family pew of Sir Robert Melville of Burntisland. It is closely comparable to one in the great church in Breda, Holland, as adapted for protestant worship. The building was used for the General Assembly of the Church of Scotland in 1601, at which the preparation of what became the Authorised Version of the Bible in English was initiated. Today there is still a sense in this church of the renewed vigour in church life that came with the Reformation, and of the reinvigorated connections with northern Europe which sharing reformed Christianity gave to Scotland. Central planning on this scale shows how prosperous the port of Burntisland was in the late sixteenth century. The experiment was not, however, repeated in this form, probably because there were problems with sight lines and acoustic problems, but possibly also because worship practice in Scotland after the Union of the Crowns in 1603 moved away from the Dutch model to the Danish Lutheran one. The church still sits above the harbour of Burntisland, a landmark to navigators, as well as a place of worship.

34. *St Quivox Parish Church, Auchincruive*

*T*his church is on a knoll, suggesting that it is on an early worship site. Though it incorporates parts of a medieval church, St Quivox is in its present form unequivocally presbyterian in form and layout. It was originally rectangular in plan and said to have been built in 1595. The belfry dates from the seventeenth century, and the body of the building took its present form in 1767, when it was repaired and a north aisle was added by the Oswalds of Auchincruive, the principal heritors. The present rectangular windows probably date from the 1760s alterations. The interior is simply furnished. There is a fine Greek Revival mausoleum in the graveyard, built for the Campbells of Craigie and Bardarroch.

35. *Dirleton Parish Church*

*T*his a thoroughly delightful building, in a wonderful sheltered, wooded setting, its warm reddish sandstone walls contrasting with the rich greenness of the well-kept graveyard grass and the dark yew trees. While Burntisland is a product of a mercantile Scots burgh, Dirleton, built in about 1615, epitomises the influence on a rural parish of a major landed family, in this case the owners of the Archerfield estate. This part of East Lothian was noted for its cereal crops, which made the landowners among the wealthiest in Scotland. The tall bell tower reflects the Church of Scotland's emphasis on the use of bells as a call to worship. The shell of the building appears to be remarkably little altered, apart from the construction of a burial aisle in 1664 for James Maxwell, Earl of Dirleton, on the south wall, and the rebuilding of the parapet of the tower in 1836. The so-called Archerfield Aisle is an example of the blending of classical and Romanesque revival architecture. The village of Dirleton, dominated by its great castle, is evocative of the nature of medieval settlement in lowland Scotland, though it is now a home for the wealthy rather than an estate village.

36. Cawdor Parish Church

*T*he only surviving parts of the parish church built in 1619 are the tall bell tower, with its unusual battlemented top and plate-traceried south window, and the porch diagonally set in the north-east angle of the cruciform building. The inset belfry stage on the tower was probably added in about 1830, as the body of the church was built in 1829–30 by John Wilson, mason, and John McIntosh, wright. The interior fittings date from 1904, when the layout was recast to designs by John Wittet. There are galleries in the north, east and west aisles, with gothic-detailed fronts. The pulpit is similarly detailed. Like Dirleton, Cawdor is essentially an estate village, and this is essentially a landowner's church. The tower is an unusual feature in an early seventeenth-century church.

37. Greyfriars Tolbooth and Highland Kirk, Edinburgh

*A*s with Burntisland, Greyfriars was a one-off, perhaps experimental church, as originally conceived. The building was constructed to serve the expanding southern suburbs of Edinburgh. Construction began in 1602, using material from a convent at Sciennes, about half a mile to the south, but the first campaign ended in 1604. Building was resumed in 1612, and was completed in 1620. The church was built on a rectangular plan, with aisles on both sides, and a bell tower at the west end. This medieval layout was not, however, apparently designed to be used with an 'east end'. Instead, the planning of the church appears to have been based on Dutch adaptations of pre-Reformation churches for their form of reformed worship, with the pulpit on one of the long sides of the main part of the church. It seems likely – in view of the signing of the National Covenant in Greyfriars Churchyard in 1638, in protest against the Anglicanisation of worship in Scotland – that Greyfriars church was a focus for residents of Edinburgh who favoured Dutch-style worship practices, as opposed to the Danish-Lutheran form of worship which had, it seems likely, been introduced, with episco-pacy, by James VI in 1610. The building was used as a barracks between 1650 and 1653, but then reverted to use as a church. In 1718 gunpowder stored in the tower exploded, badly damaging the west end of the building. A wall was built at the west end of the four undamaged bays, to allow worship to continue, and a new church – New Greyfriars – was built on to the west end, the remains of the tower being demolished. The two damaged western bays were repaired, and two more added. The architect, Alexander McGill, also added a north porch. In 1845 a fire in Old Greyfriars gutted that section, and destroyed the furnishings in New Greyfriars. The arcades in Old Greyfriars were demolished later in the 1840s, and in 1856–7 the building was re-roofed by David Cousin as an aisle-less space. The two congregations united in 1929, and between 1931 and 1938 the church was rebuilt as a single space, with the arcades replaced and the east and west fronts restored. In recent years the interior has again been reordered, with seats replacing pews, allowing for flexibility in ordering worship. The church sits in a large graveyard, laid out in 1622, and subsequently enlarged. It contains an unrivalled group of monuments, mausolea and grave enclosures, testifying to the exceptional wealth of the city in the seventeenth and eighteenth centuries. The mausolea of the Adam family of architects, and of Alexander Mackenzie of Rosehaugh (designed by James Smith) are particularly notable.

38. *Anstruther Parish Church, Anstruther Easter*

*T*his is a large church for its period, and a well-detailed one, its scale reflecting the importance at the time of the burghs of the East Neuk of Fife as trading ports. It was built in 1634 as a chapel of ease of the parish church of Kilrenny, to the east, the former position of which was being usurped by the burgh of Anstruther Easter. It is built on a T-plan, with a western tower added in 1644. The tower is unusual in having an external stair turret, with cap-house, on its north-west corner. It was altered in 1834, and the three-light windows, with round heads, may date from that time, The church was reordered in 1905, by McArthy and Watson, in a disappointingly dull manner. The nearby manse predates the church, and is the oldest building still used as a manse in the Church of Scotland. The tower was probably built, in part, as a navigational aid for vessels using the harbour.

1. Brechin Cathedral and Round Tower (1). This view, from the south east, shows the slender round tower on the left, which dates from the eleventh century. Its design is Irish influenced. The choir of the cathedral, which was restored in 1900–2, is on the right.

2. Glasgow Cathedral (3). Scotland's greatest surviving mediaeval church is seen here from the east. The lower tier of windows lights the remarkable lower church, housing the shrine of the founder. Above are the windows of the passage which allowed pilgrims to walk round outside the choir.

3. Paisley Abbey (7). The only part of the Abbey church to survive intact is the nave, with this great West Door dating from the early thirteenth century, superbly elegant in its use of multiple receding arched mouldings to give a sense of importance to the actual doors.

4. St Athernase's Parish Church, Leuchars (8).

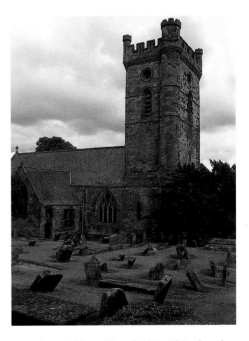

5. Culross Abbey Church (12). This church took its present form in about 1500, when the nave of the Cistercian abbey church was demolished. The tower and north aisle, seen here, were built instead on top of the stone screens which had separated the nave from the choir.

6. St Machar's Cathedral, Aberdeen (16). This west front is arguably the finest surviving mediaeval facade in Scotland. The slender round-headed lights in the west window are unique in Scottish churches of the period.

7. St Monan's Parish Church (19). Set beside the sea, the interior of this small fourteenth-century church has a calm solidity speaking of many generations of worship. This is one of two ship models hanging in the church, a three-decker man of war.

8. St Michael's Parish Church, Linlithgow (21). St Michael's is one of the great Scots late mediaeval parish churches. The original imperial crown steeple, like that at King's College Chapel (30), was removed in about 1821. This dramatic aluminium-clad replacement was installed in 1964.

9. Kilbirnie Auld Kirk (25). The Crawfurd (Crawford) Loft, built for Viscount Garnock in about 1705, is the most remarkable piece of early eighteenth-century woodwork in any Scots church, and has recently been restored. It is decorated with armorial panels relating to the Crawfurds.

10. St Columba's Parish Church, Burntisland (33). This view shows the north east corner of the church, with two of the masonry piers supporting the roof and belfry, and the Melville (Magistrates') pew. The model on the right is of the Great Michael, the largest ship of the Scots navy.

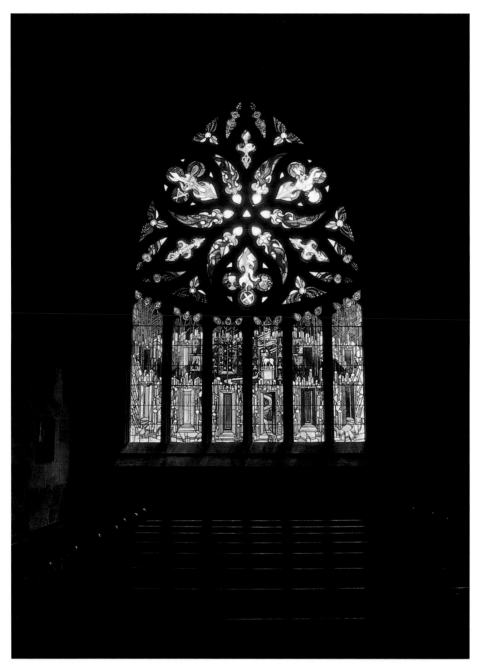

11. St Michael's Parish Church, Linlithgow (21A). Set in the south chapel, this is said to be 'the most beautiful Late Gothic window in Scotland', with its entrancing geometric and loop tracery. The glass is by Crear McCartney, installed in 1992 to mark the 750th anniversary of the church.

12. Dalserf Parish Church (49). The body of this distinctive parish church dates from 1655, but was remodelled in 1721. The central projection with its elongated cast-iron belfry was added in 1892, giving the building an unusual elegance.

13. King's College Chapel, Aberdeen (30). One of the two surviving pre-Reformation crown steeples in Scotland, this one emphasises the Royal status of one of Aberdeen' two University colleges. The imperial crown was appropriated by the later Stewart monarchs as a symbol of ascendancy.

14. St Columba's Parish Church, Burntisland (32). This unique square building was one of the first Reformed churches in Scotland, opened in 1592. The central belfry was later replaced in stone and the walls heightened in 1822. The open stair on the right leads to the Sailors' Loft.

39. Kirkmaiden Parish Church

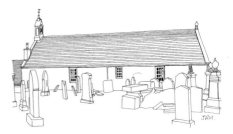

A long, low building, constructed in 1638 at the centre of a large rural parish, Kirkmaiden is probably more typical of seventeenth-century churches than Anstruther, and has escaped the raising of the wall-heads which has altered the character of many older churches. The almost domestic rectangular windows are typical of many churches built from the early seventeenth to late eighteenth century, and are probably a reaction against the pointed windows of the pre-Reformation Gothic: an explicit statement that this is a Reformed church. The bellcote was built in 1885, probably a replacement for an earlier one, at the same time as the interior was refitted. The north jamb was built as the burial aisle of the McDoualls of Logan, and, as part of the 1885 refitting, a gallery was installed on top of the burial vault. The church is in a small hamlet, typical of the setting of many rural parish churches which were built near the geographical centre of a scattered agricultural community. The graveyard contains a grave marker in the form of a miniature lighthouse in memory of James Scott, son of a keeper of the Mull of Galloway lighthouse.

40. Fenwick Parish Church

T his is an early example, built in 1643, of a church planned as an equal-armed (Greek) cross. This type of design was apparently associated with a form of worship linked to Danish Lutheranism, with one arm of the cross used as a Communion aisle, so that for a preaching service the building probably functioned as a T-plan structure. The steeply-pitched roof may originally have been thatched. There are external stairs to galleries. The pointed windows represent the survival of traces of Gothic, and hint at the adherence of the landowning family to episcopal forms, rather than to the more extreme protestant approach to worship and belief represented by Kirkmaiden. The belfry, added in 1660, was reconstructed in 1864, and the interior was rebuilt after a fire in 1929 to designs by Gabriel Steel of Kilmarnock. At the entrances to the churchyard there are little 'sentry boxes', built in 1828, to house elders collecting offerings from worshippers. At the time of its construction

Fenwick was an estate village, but in the eighteenth century it became a centre for the hand-loom weaving of linen, and later cotton. The present form of the settlement dates from that period.

41. Lyne Parish Church

This little church, constructed in 1640–5, is in an upland, and always sparsely-populated, part of Peebles-shire but, like Stobo (see above), it is close to an important through route from Lanarkshire to the eastern borders. There was an earlier church here, probably from the twelfth century, when it was a chapel of Stobo. Unlike Kirkmaiden which is obviously presbyterian in design, Lyne, with its Reformed Gothic survival details, shows traces of having been arranged for east-end Communion. The two eastern windows on the south front have cuspless tracery with a loop in the head, a feature of one of the windows in Stobo. A belfry was added in 1708. The building was restored in 1888, when the belfry was rebuilt and a porch and two west-end buttresses were added. The interior dates largely from 1888, but the circular, panelled pulpit and two oak canopied pews survive from the building's construction. The pews were apparently built for Lord John Hay of Yester, the heritor, and his wife. The medieval font was recovered from the demolition of an internal wall. The base is modern. The church is still set in open countryside and, despite the Victorian porch and belfry, can still evoke the atmosphere of a part of seventeenth-century Scotland where religious conservatism had not been overtaken by reforming zeal.

42. Ayr Old Parish Church (The Auld Kirk of Ayr)

This is another church on a Greek-cross plan, built in 1653–4 and probably, like Fenwick, an expression of a particular strand of practice and belief. This is a burgh church, so it is on a larger scale than Fenwick. Ayr was one of the most important west of Scotland ports at the time of its construction, and also a garrison town. The church is not a notably elegant building, but it makes up for that with its interest as the only church of its period still in use. It was paid for by the Commonwealth Government and, if my analysis of its design is correct, its design reflects the religious tolerance of Cromwell's regime. Extreme protestantism was more a rural than an urban phenomenon. It was designed by Theophilius Rankeine, but in 1836 it was altered by David Bryce, who replaced its original canvas ceiling with pitch pine, and rebuilt the dormer windows, doubling their number. Further alterations were made in the later nineteenth and early twentieth centuries. During the 1860s reordering, a suite of stained-glass windows was installed. In 1952 the building was restored, reversing the worst of the inappropriate Victorian and later interventions, but retaining the stained glass. The original pulpit has been restored. The three galleries are supported on turned wooden columns. Round the walls are some fine classical mural monuments. The approach to the church from the high street is through a stone lych gate, built in 1626, a rare feature in Scotland. Because it predates the church, it may have been constructed as the entrance to the burial ground in which the church is set.

43. *Lauder Old Parish Church*

*L*ike Fenwick, this is a landowner's church built on a Greek-cross plan. The heritor responsible for its construction, in 1673, was the powerful Duke of Lauderdale, effective ruler of Scotland at the time, whose nearby house, Thirlestane Castle, was one of the first recognisably modern mansions in Scotland. This church was built to replace one in the grounds of the castle and was designed by Sir William Bruce, the first recognisably modern architect in Scotland. The church has a central octagonal belfry. Internally, one of the arms of the cross was certainly a Communion aisle. All the arms are now seated, and there is a splendid pulpit of 1820 with a massive sounding board on one of the angles. The windows are round-headed, with intersecting-arc tracery. The whole effect is of decency and simplicity, a contrast to the behaviour of the Duke of Lauderdale, a venial man in a venial age. At the time of the building of the church, Lauder was essentially an estate village. Later it grew as a weaving settlement, and as a staging post for coaches travelling between Edinburgh and the Borders towns and further south.

44. Greenlaw Parish Church

*A*lmost an exact contemporary of Lauder Old, Greenlaw represents the other main strand in seventeenth-century church design, being a long rectangle in plan, with the pulpit at the centre of the south long wall, and galleries at each end. The eastern section of the building dates from 1675. As mentioned in connection with Kirkmaiden, the rectangular plan probably relates to a Dutch-influenced, rather than Danish-influenced, form of worship, with Communion celebrated on a table in front of the pulpit, rather than in a separate section of the building. The long rectangular plan may, however, relate to a pre-Reformation church on the site, for Greenlaw is an ancient settlement. The tower at the west end was originally detached, and was built in 1696 by the burgh, which was for many years the county town of Berwickshire. The building served as the lock-up for local malefactors, as well as a clock tower and belfry, and still retains its barred windows and a fine yett (door grille). The shaft of the old mercat cross, a Corinthian column, dating from 1609, is now mounted on the west wall of the tower. The church was extended to the west in 1712 to meet the tower. A north aisle was added in 1855 opposite the pulpit, making the plan into a T. The building was refurnished in 1833. It has a plastered wagon roof, and the gallery fronts are panelled and painted. The pulpit remains in the centre of the long south wall. The burgh of Greenlaw did not develop on the scale of other Borders towns and the central grouping of church, classical former County Buildings (1829), and the contemporary Castle Inn, with extensive stabling and coach houses (built to accommodate people of importance frequenting the county town), look out of proportion to the size of what is now just a village.

45. St Andrew's Parish Church, Tongue

*I*t is remarkable that a building on this scale could be built in Sutherland in the late seventeenth and early eighteenth century, and it is evidence of the strength of the local economy in the period before industrialisation and agricultural improvement. Tongue is on a natural harbour, a ferry point for communication along the north coast of Scotland, and on a practicable route from the coast to the interior of Sutherland. It is very likely that Tongue had, by the standards of the time, an extensive trade in imported goods and in the export of agricultural goods. The church, first built in 1680, was substantially rebuilt in 1728–9, and the interior was remodelled in 1861–2, when the present belfry was constructed. The Reay Loft, possibly of 1728–9, is now in the National Museums of Scotland. The building is modest enough by later standards, but it is well built and proportioned, and has an endearing simplicity, reinforced by the limewashing of its rubble walls.

46. Canongate Parish Church, Edinburgh

A church with a most unusual history, the Canongate replaced the nave of the former Holyrood Abbey as the burgh church of the Canongate when James VII, as Duke of York, claimed the abbey church as his Roman Catholic Chapel Royal. The new building was constructed in 1688–91 with the assistance of a mortification (legacy) from Thomas Moodie, left for the purpose of building a church in the Grassmarket. The architect of the Canongate Church was James Smith, who also designed the adaptation of the abbey church. It was built on the site of a group of the typical gabled houses which lined the Canongate, and of the gardens laid out on 'burgage plots' running down to the valley at the foot of the Calton Hill, with the rest of the gardens forming a graveyard, laid out at the same time as the church was built. The site is next to the Canongate Tolbooth, the administrative centre of the burgh. The church has a curvilinear gable facing the street, with a classical porch. Between the tall, round-headed, central windows are the arms of Thomas Moodie above a plaque recording his benefaction. Above these windows is a central, circular one, and above that are the arms of William III, who was king by the time the church was completed. At the apex of the gable are the antlers of a deer, which are renewed from time to time from the royal estates at Balmoral. The body of the church is on a cruciform plan, with an aisled nave, and a small semicircular apse, and was intended for episcopal worship. The suggestion has been made that the building was designed for easy conversion to Roman Catholic worship, but this seems unlikely, in view of the opposition of Edinburgh to James VII and his Romanising ambitions. I believe that it was, in fact, designed for Danish-Lutheran worship, like the Greek-cross-plan churches mentioned above. The apse was walled off and a central pulpit installed in the eighteenth century, but the church was opened up between 1946 and 1954 when the building was restored by Ian G. Lindsay and Partners. The side (east and west) galleries were removed at that time, and the south gallery was lowered. The pulpit dates from 1847, and came from the Territorial Free Church. The sounding board was made in 1961, to a design by Esmé Gordon. The resulting interior is remarkably light and airy with its large clear-glazed, round-headed windows, a forerunner of what became the typical Georgian church of the later eighteenth century.

47. *Durisdeer Parish Church*

*W*hilst the Canongate church is a pre-eminently urban building, Durisdeer is entirely rural, set in a hamlet on the edge of the hill country of the Southern Uplands, and still a place to be sought out rather than encountered by chance. It seems to have been an ancient place of worship, but the existing buildings are of the late seventeenth century. There is a connection with the Canongate: the leading heritors of the parish, the Dukes of Queensberry, were also leading residents of the burgh of Canongate. The oldest part of the Durisdeer complex is the burial aisle of the Queensberry family. This was built on to a medieval parish church for the interment of the first duke in 1695 and designed by James Smith, with a vault covered by a marble baldacchino (canopy) modelled on one in St Peter's Church in Rome. The building was completed in 1708. After the second duke (the man who negotiated the Act of Union through the Scottish Parliament) died in 1714, his coffin, too, was placed in the vault, and a splendid monument to him and his wife was placed on the north wall of the aisle. The monument was designed by John van Nost, a Dutchman, and the leading monumental sculptor of his day. The body of the church was built in 1718–20, probably also to a design by James Smith, on a T-plan, with a two-storey retiring room for the duke at the end of its west wing. The ducal residence, Drumlanrig Castle, is at a considerable distance from the church. The tower was added in 1729. The building was remodelled in 1784, and again in the early nineteenth century, when the present pulpit was installed. It was moved to its present location in about 1870. There are few more surprising churches in Scotland: to find architecture and monumental sculpture of such sophistication in such a remote place is utterly unexpected.

48. *Yester Parish Church, Gifford*

*D*urisdeer is a 'one-off', while Yester is on first inspection a 'typical Scottish country church', with its white harling, round-headed Georgian windows, T-plan, and chunky tower with short, slated steeple. All is not, however, what it seems. Yester is a product of successive alterations. The first church here was built in 1710 to replace the early medieval St Bothan's Church when its site was included in the grounds of Yester House. The plan and lower walls are of that date, designed like Durisdeer and Yester House by James Smith, but the walls were heightened in 1830, when the windows flanking the pulpit gained their round heads. The interior was remodelled at the same time, with a new pulpit with sounding board, box pews and panelled gallery fronts. The north aisle contains the Tweeddale gallery, which has the arms of the family on a central panel, and which has its own external stair to a lugged doorway. The chancel area is delineated by low, pierced, wooden partitions. The general effect is immensely pleasing. The church is a prominent feature of the pretty village of Gifford, though its contribution to the townscape has been reduced by the planting of trees in front of it. These have now grown to the point where it is difficult to have a clear view of this interesting and important building.

49. *Dalserf Parish Church*

*T*his church may well be on an ancient site, but it apparently began to take its present form in 1655. It was enlarged in 1721 into a T-plan structure, the typical layout for churches in Scotland for much of the eighteenth century. As at Fenwick (see above), the galleries have external stairs. It escaped further modernisation until the late nineteenth century, as the community it served was not affected by the industrialisation which characterised so much of Lanarkshire from the early nineteenth century. When alterations were eventually made, they took the form of a central south wing surmounted by a tall, cast-iron belfry with an ogee roof, giving the building an instantly recognisable silhouette. The scale of the addition does not, however, seriously affect the early eighteenth-century character of the building. Its setting, too, is largely unspoiled, though the village cottages, thatched until the 1950s, now have slate roofs.

50. St Andrew's Parish Church, Golspie

This is one of the least altered mid-eighteenth-century churches in Scotland. It was built in 1732 as the estate church for the Earls (later Dukes) of Sutherland, replacing a seventeenth-century building, and its scale indicates that at that time east Sutherland was reasonably prosperous. It was originally T-plan, but a wing was added in 1754 to make it cruciform. It has the rectangular windows typical of most of the churches of the period. The bellcote was added in 1774. Internally, the most prominent feature is the private gallery of the Sutherland family, with a retiring room behind, built by Kenneth Sutherland in 1738 at the same time as the pulpit. The gallery is exceptionally elegant, with two tiers of three wooden, Roman-Doric columns supporting the gallery front and a richly-detailed entablature featuring the Sutherland arms in the centre. The front and the walls of the space behind are simply panelled. The Dukes of Sutherland became notorious in the nineteenth century for their association with the Highland Clearances, but this church has no connection with this troubled period in Scottish history. The church was restored in 1953–4 to designs by George Hay, and the present box pews were installed by him at that time. It is a very satisfying building, the epitome of the plain, unadorned parish church. The dignified simplicity of the Sutherland loft is entirely in keeping with the rest of the building. The village of Golspie was remodelled on a regular plan in the early nineteenth century by the Sutherland Estates.

51. Hamilton Old Parish Church

*H*amilton Old shares with Golspie an aristocratic connection and a cruciform plan, but that is the only similarity. The Hamilton church was built in 1732 by the then Duke of Hamilton as a burgh church for his town of Hamilton and, in keeping with the Duke's sense of his status, was designed by the leading architect of the day, William Adam. It is on a Greek-cross plan, but unlike the seventeenth-century churches already mentioned has a central, circular space, surmounted by a glazed rotunda. The main entrances are at the ends of the north and south arms of the cross, with triple-arched doorways. The interior of the church was substantially remodelled in 1926, and now features embroidery by Hannah Frew Paterson and engraved glass by Anita Pate. Part of the original pulpit survives. Outside the north entrance the Netherton Cross, a tenth-century cross with interlace decoration, has been set. It was formerly in Hamilton Low Parks, probably on the site of the earliest centre of Christian worship in the neighbourhood. The church halls, to the south of the church, are in a very pleasant, unassertive, Scots Renaissance building of 1886. A new road has been sliced through the town past the churchyard, and some brutal new buildings have been built beside the road, overlooking the church and its graveyard, which remains, with the buildings of the Low Parks Museum, and the mausoleum, reminders of the days when Hamilton was a ducal seat. The palace itself was demolished in the 1920s, though the ducal hunting lodge at Chatelherault survives at Fernigair, south of the burgh.

52. Kilmarnock Old High Parish Church

*L*ike Hamilton Old, this is a very advanced building for its period, a broad rectangular building which anticipates in its layout many of the great urban churches of the mid and late eighteenth century. It was built in 1732–40 at a time when Kilmarnock was emerging as the leading trading centre of northern Ayrshire, and complemented the old Laigh (low) Church to the south. The building has, like many of its successors, two tiers of windows, and a horse-shoe gallery. The windows have Gibbs surrounds, a very up-to-date feature. The most striking feature of the building is, however, the tower, with its elegant cupola, the first of its kind in Scotland. The church is set in a large, walled graveyard, and has since 1848 been overshadowed by the Kilmarnock Viaduct of the Glasgow, Paisley, Kilmarnock and Ayr Railway, which also cuts off the building from the town centre. The external stonework is not in good condition, but the building remains a most elegant feature of Kilmarnock's townscape, and occupies an important place in the history of church building in eighteenth-century Scotland.

53. *Crossmichael Parish Church*

Crossmichael is an agricultural-improvement village at the south end of Loch Ken, at the point where east-west and north-south routes through the Stewartry of Kirkcudbright intersect. The church is on a knoll at the north end of the village, probably on an ancient worship site. Its most conspicuous feature is the round tower attached to the south side, a notable landmark. The body of the church was originally built between 1749 and 1751 on the site of an earlier building, on a T-plan. The lower part of the tower may be a survival from that building, perhaps dating back to 1611. There was a major rebuilding in 1822–3, by David McLellan, involving the addition of a north jamb. The windows were probably given their pointed heads at the same time, and the present galleries and pews were installed. There are heritors' box pews in the south corners which date from the original mid-eighteenth-century building. The tower was heightened in 1824–5, and the spire added. In the churchyard is a remarkably-elaborate, classical monument to William Gordon of Greenlaw, who died in 1752, erected by his wife.

54. *Lunnasting Parish Church, Lunna*

This is a very unusual church in a remote part of mainland Shetland, constructed in 1753 on a scale appropriate to this sparsely-populated area. Internally, it is typical of its period, with the pulpit on one of the long walls, and pews crowding round it. The pulpit is hexagonal, with panelled sides and a circular sounding board. Like that at Tingwall (see below), the underside of the sounding board is panelled in a redial pattern, a distinctive Shetland feature. The U-plan gallery is supported on wooden Tuscan columns. The east and west galleries have panelled fronts, but the north gallery has a balustrated front, probably to allow worshippers to see the Communion table. Externally, the most distinctive feature is a range of buttresses on the pulpit wall, apparently out of proportion to the scale of the building. The purpose of these is obscure, but it has recently been suggested that they were built as part of a heating system. This little, white-harled church with its unique built form is a striking feature in the almost treeless Shetland landscape. It is close to a small natural harbour, probably used by worshippers, and to a circular limekiln.

55. *St Nicholas' Parish Church, Aberdeen*

This was the medieval burgh church of Aberdeen, and one of the largest of its kind. The first church on the site was built before 1151, and the surviving north transept (Collison's Aisle) dates from the late twelfth century. The church was rebuilt on a larger scale in the fifteenth century, and the choir was underbuilt, as in Glasgow Cathedral and in the church of the Holy Rude, Stirling. The under-building, constructed in 1438 by Sir Andrew Wrycht, survives under the east church as St Mary's Chapel. After the Reformation, as in other churches of its kind, the choir and nave were separated to cater for two congregations; unlike in others, this arrangement persisted until the late twentieth century, though by that time both parts had been completely rebuilt – the nave (the west church) in 1755, and the east in about 1837. This left the crossing, transepts and St Mary's Chapel (restored in 1898 by Dr William Kelly) as the only reasonably-unaltered parts of the pre-Reformation church. The west church, on the site of the former nave, which had fallen into decay by the early eighteenth century, is the more remarkable, as the only Scottish work of James Gibbs, Aberdeen's greatest architect, who practised mainly in London. The design was presented to the city in 1741 by Gibbs after the town council made him an honorary burgess in 1739, but the church was not built until 1752–5. It has a barrel-vaulted central section with flanking round-arched arcades, supporting side galleries. Externally, this structure is expressed by the central section protruding above the aisles. The pedimented gable at the west-end has a central, 'Gibbs surround' arched window, and a rusticated porch below. The sloping sub-gables of the aisles are set back. At the west end is the Town's Loft, still used by the City Council for the Kirking of the Council, and the east end is now the organ loft. The pulpit is in the centre of the south side of the central space, and has an enormous sounding board. The galleries and box pews are Gibbs' originals. The general impression of the interior is of calm solidity. The medieval choir, like the east church, was restored and recased in 1835–7 by Archibald Simpson, but was destroyed in a spectacular fire in 1875, which also burned the sixteenth-century lead-covered timber spire. The east church and the spire were rebuilt in 1875–7 to designs by William Smith, as a fairly conventional Gothic Revival structure. A chapel has recently been created in the north transept as a memorial to men who have lost their lives while working in the North Sea oil industry, with a fine stained-glass window. The church is set in a large graveyard, with some exceptionally fine monuments, an oasis of calm in the busy city centre. A monumental classical screen wall, designed by John Smith and built in 1829, separates the churchyard from Union Street, here carried on a series of arches over sloping ground.

56. *Mearns Parish Church, Newton Mearns*

*O*nce a country church, serving a largely agricultural parish, Mearns has been almost, but not quite, swamped by suburban development. Enough survives of its wooded setting, however, to give a feel of its original character. The building probably derives its elegant bell tower, with elongated ogee cap, from c. 1755, and the form of its body, with the tall round-headed windows flanking the tower, from 1813. The bell tower is broader than it is deep, an unusual feature. The porches, interior fittings and roof-ridge ventilator date from the 1920s. The gatepiers are hollowed out, to serve as shelters for elders collecting offerings.

57. *St Ninian's Catholic Chapel, Tynet*

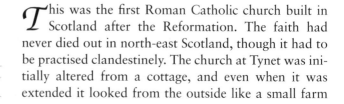

*T*his was the first Roman Catholic church built in Scotland after the Reformation. The faith had never died out in north-east Scotland, though it had to be practised clandestinely. The church at Tynet was initially altered from a cottage, and even when it was extended it looked from the outside like a small farm steading, as it still does. It was originally thatched, but is now slated. Built in 1755 and extended in 1787 and about 1800, it later fell into decay. It was restored in 1951 by Ian G. Lindsay and Partners. The tiny sanctuary with its diminutive classical ambo (pulpit) and wooden altar rails is most moving: a reminder of faithfulness in the face of persecution.

58. Fogo Parish Church

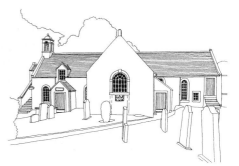

*T*his little country parish church, constructed in stages from 1755, preserves much of the atmosphere of an earlier, simpler, if harder age, both internally and externally. Its small scale and simple, almost austere fittings are a reminder of life in rural Scotland before it was touched by industrialisation, improved communications, and thoroughgoing agricultural improvement. The body of the building was constructed in about 1755, and incorporates a seventeenth-century burial aisle. The church was 'repaired' in 1817, probably the date of the fittings, and was enlarged in 1853. Though not of one date, the complex forms a satisfyingly irregular composition, set in a farming landscape not entirely alien to that in which it was originally built.

59. Oakshaw Trinity Church, Paisley

*N*ow known as Oakshaw Trinity Church, as a result of a series of unions with other churches, the building of this church, originally known as the High Kirk, was undertaken when the adapted nave of the Abbey could no longer cope with the expanding population of Paisley, which was a booming textile town. The church was built on a broad rectangular plan in 1756, without any internal supports for the roof, which had, it is said, the largest span in Scotland at the time. It had a horse-shoe gallery from the start. Like the near-contemporary Mid Kirk at Greenock (see below), it was built without a tower or spire. The Paisley clock tower and spire were added in 1770, at the expense of the town council. The tower is of a curiously old-fashioned design, redolent of the Merchants' Steeple in Glasgow of nearly a century earlier, but the spire was very up-to-date, with glazed oval openings in its cardinal faces. The interior was completely remodelled in 1877 in an opulently Victorian style, with an elaborate ceiling rose, from which presumably a large gasolier was originally suspended. After the amalgamation which created Oakshaw Trinity, the shell of the building was repaired, and the interior refurbished and to an extent modernised, in the early 1990s. Perhaps, when the dust of integration has settled, the original descriptive and dignified name of the church might be restored in the future.

60. *Torphichen Parish Church*

*H*ere we have the juxtaposition of a medieval survival with the eighteenth-century building that replaced another part of the church as a place of worship. The medieval building consists of the crossing and transepts of the Preceptory of the Knights Hospitallers of the Order of St John, founded in the late twelfth century. In the fifteenth century the walls of the transepts and crossing were greatly heightened, and rooms were formed above the vaults, possibly as a refuge in times of trouble. After the Reformation the nave of the church served as the parish church, and the crossing and transepts were used as a court house. In 1756 the nave was dismantled, and its materials were used to build a T-plan Georgian church. This was refurnished in 1803, and the pews and galleries of that date still survive. The pulpit, with its sounding board, may be older. Some of the pews can be converted into Communion pews by an ingenious mechanism. At the time when the parish church was built, Torphichen was an agricultural village, and the impetus to build anew may well have come from agricultural improvement and the surplus this created. The remains of the preceptory are in the care of Historic Scotland.

61. *Wellpark Mid Kirk, Greenock*

*T*he town of Greenock benefited enormously from the access to the West Indies and the American colonies which followed the Act of Union in 1707. The value of this access increased after the Seven Years' War, which increased British influence in the New World. The West Kirk had been built soon after the Reformation, but the town expanded round the harbour built to accommodate the fleet trading with the colonies, and it was there that the new Mid Kirk was built in 1757. It is said that a design was obtained from

Bristol, but there are also parallels with St Andrew's Church in Glasgow, completed in 1756, and with James Gibbs' St Martin-in-the-Fields in London. The Mid Kirk was certainly one of the first churches in Scotland with a classical portico. A steeple was apparently included in the Bristol design, but it was not built until 1787 and then in a shortened version. It is more completely integrated with the church than that at Paisley. The church, appropriately, is at the top of William Street, which used to link the town centre to the Old Harbour. The harbour was filled in between the First and Second World Wars, and its site is now covered by a main road and by modern buildings, severing the visual connection between the town centre and its former lifeblood, the deep-water channel of the Clyde Estuary. The kirk itself is the best reminder of the mid-eighteenth-century prosperity of Greenock, when it was the most important port on the west coast of Scotland, though there are two buildings in William Street, built in 1752 and 1755, which are nearly contemporary with the kirk.

62. *Inverness Old High Kirk*

*T*he river Ness, as it passes through the city of Inverness, gives a spacious quality to the place, enhanced by a succession of steeples on the east bank. The oldest of these belongs to the Old High and springs from a tower, the body of which probably dates from the sixteenth century. The parapet may have been added in 1549. The spire is octagonal, with a pyramidal copper roof above a louvered bell stage. The tower dominates the body of the church, which is also simple and was built in 1769–72. The semi-octagonal gallery may date from 1840, and the pews, of modified box type, were installed in 1877–9. The present, open-timber roof was installed in 1899. The three galleries are supported on turned wooden columns. There are stained-glass windows by, among others, Ballantine and Gardiner, Douglas Strachan and Gordon Webster. The building was remodelled in 1891 by local architects Ross and Macbeth, with porches and an apse. Though a conspicuous feature from the river side, the building has little presence from the town side, since it is hidden by a row of houses, the entrance being set back and sandwiched between secular buildings. On the east side of the building is the Robertson burial enclosure of 1660, with a Corinthianesque colonnade supporting a deep Renaissance entablature. The frieze is liberally ornamented with skulls and crossbones and other emblems of mortality. The enclosure contains a fine, late seventeenth-century mural monument. This is arguably the finest seventeenth-century grave enclosure in Scotland.

63. *Kilarrow Parish Church, Bowmore*

*A*t Bowmore, on the isle of Islay, at the top of the main street of this eighteenth-century planned town, Kilarrow is the only complete circular church in Scotland. It was built in 1767–9 for David Campbell of Shawfield and Islay, to replace the old church of Kilarrow, near Islay House, and was designed as the focal point of the new planned town. The circular form was chosen when central planning was being revived as a concept. Externally, the church is virtually unaltered, but a gallery was added in 1830, and it was refurnished in the late nineteenth century. The reason why the model was not repeated is obvious: the massive, central, wooden column supporting the conical roof obstructs sight-lines from much of the back of the church.

64. *St Andrew's Parish Church, Dundee*

*B*uilt in 1774–7 as the church of the Incorporated Trades of Dundee, on a commanding site, St Andrew's has a spire roughly similar to that of Paisley High Kirk. However, the body of the church is treated in a much more fashionable manner, with Venetian windows and swags enlivening the south, show front. The approach to the building from the street is up a broad flight of steps, and through a generously-proportioned set of gates with gatepiers installed in 1810 and modified in 1828. When the church was built, Dundee was a notable port, and also a growing centre of linen manufacture. Like Aberdeen, it also provided services to a large and prosperous hinterland. The setting of the building is remarkably open for an urban church, and its lively detailing gives it a very cheerful – and not obviously presbyterian – aspect. One suspects that the commissioning body, and the architect, Samuel Bell, had seen some of the Wren churches in the City of London. The design is said to have been adapted from one by James Craig, the author of the plan for Edinburgh's first New Town. The interior was restored in 1939, and has a semi-octagonal gallery supported on six Doric columns. The gallery fronts are decorated with the emblems of the incorporated trades, and the building also contains the banners and ceremonial chairs of the nine trades. The pulpit is panelled, with an Ionic pedimented backboard. The stained glass includes work by William Wilson, Gordon Webster and Douglas Hogg. Immediately to the east is the former Glasite chapel, built at the same time as St Andrew's. The Glasites were the first group to secede from the Church of Scotland in the eighteenth century (see Introduction). The building was refurbished in the 1960s by Thom and Wilkie, and serves as halls for St Andrew's.

65. *Irvine Old Parish Church*

*T*his is another large burgh church with a classical steeple, like the Mid Kirk, Greenock and Dundee St Andrew's built for a congregation in a prosperous port. Irvine Old was built in 1774, and it was designed to look in two directions: north to the town, with a frontage not unlike that of the High Kirk of Paisley, and west across the river Irvine to the sea, with large windows that were originally clear-glazed. The interior was refurnished in 1897. This church is a more convincing overall composition than the others mentioned, and shares with the Old High, Inverness, the advantage of a riverside setting. It is the most majestic of this generation of churches. Irvine was the last of Scotland's New Towns to be designated, and one of the first parts to be built was a new shopping centre, constructed on a bridge over the river Irvine. Though it was built with good intentions, it destroyed one of the finest urban views in west central Scotland, which was of a group of three church spires, including Irvine Old, and a low-level bridge over the river.

66. *Dyke Parish Church*

*B*uilt in 1781 for a rural parish in Moray (at that time Elginshire), Dyke is one of the first of the smaller Georgian churches with extensive glazing, probably made possible by the expansion of glass-making in the second half of the eighteenth century. Dyke's sequence of large, round-headed, clear-glazed windows is still striking. Internally, there is an impressive 'three-decker' pulpit, for minister, precentor and session clerk, on one long wall. The precentor's role was to lead the congregational singing. The original horse-shoe gallery also survives, though a ceiling has been inserted at gallery level. At one end of the building is an early to mid-eighteenth-century mausoleum which was converted into a church hall and vestry in 1948. The Gothic porch between the mausoleum and the eighteenth-century church was added in 1853. The war memorial gate arch was designed by Peter MacGregor Chalmers, and built in 1921–2. Dyke is a straggling village on an irregular plan, probably pre-Improvement in origin.

67. *Kilmodan Parish Church, Clachan of Glendaruel*

This is the second of a group of classical churches built in Argyll in the late eighteenth and early nineteenth centuries. The first, the Lowland Church in Campbeltown, had only been completed three years earlier; it has now been converted into flats. The Kilmodan church, constructed in 1783, replaced a medieval one on an adjacent site. It is on a T-plan, with a pedimented south front. An unusual feature is the provision of small circular windows flanking the pulpit. There is a belfry on the pediment. Internally, the building was renovated in 1937 and again in 1984. It retains its original layout, with central octagonal pulpit on the south wall, and three galleries with plain panelled fronts, each of which was a laird's loft for one of the three leading families in the parish. The front pews have long Communion tables in front of them. The existence in the churchyard of a number of late medieval, carved graveslabs of the characteristic West-Highland type is further evidence of both the earlier use of the site for worship and of the economic importance of the glen in the later medieval period. The best of these slabs have been placed under cover and are in the care of Historic Scotland. The remains of pre-Improvement farms can be seen on the hills which border the glen, which is now sparsely populated.

68. *St Andrew's and St George's Parish Church, Edinburgh*

This was the first church in the New Town of Edinburgh, and is on the north side of George Street, the middle street in the New Town as conceived by James Craig. It was originally intended to be built on the east side of St Andrew's Square, where the Royal Bank of Scotland is now sited, in a house built for Sir Laurence Dundas. The elliptical body (another attempt at central planning – see Kilarrow above) and classical portico were designed by Major Andrew Frazer, of the Royal Engineers, and built in 1782–4. The steeple was added in 1787 by Alexander Stevens, probably to Frazer's design. The effect is undeniably impressive, but the steeple is too tall for the rest of the building. The oval interior, though refurnished, works very well. The curved gallery is original, as is the plaster ceiling. The pulpit has been remodelled on several occasions, most recently in 1984. There are stained-glass windows by Ballantine and Co., Alfred Webster and Douglas Strachan. In 1970 the underbuilding was remodelled by Robert Hurd and Partners to provide ancillary accommodation for congregational outreach. This is now the only building in the eastern end of George Street that recalls its first, late eighteenth-century heyday, but the strength of the planning of the New Town has allowed it to absorb the many alterations that have taken place.

69. *Kilmany Parish Church*

In deeply-rural north Fife, Kilmany, dating from 1786, is typical of a number of smaller parish churches built from the 1780s to the 1800s, some on a T-plan, others on a long rectangular plan, with the pulpit on the south long wall. They differ from earlier eighteenth-century churches of similar character by having round heads to their larger windows, usually the windows flanking the pulpit. There were originally three doors on the south front of the building, one at each end, and a central one for the minister. The west and central ones have been converted into windows. Kilmany retains its original pulpit, while the box pews date from 1860. The church's particular interest lies in the ministry there of the Rev. Thomas Chalmers, who went from Kilmany to Glasgow, where he attacked the issue of the relief of urban poverty with some success. He then went on to lead the evangelical party in the Church of Scotland, and was the chief architect of the Disruption in 1843, when the evangelicals walked out of the General Assembly and established the Free Church. Kilmany preserves its rural setting among the rolling hills of north Fife, and Chalmers would still recognise it and its little village.

70. *Killean and Kilchenzie Parish Church, A'Chleit*

This is the finest of a series of simplified neoclassical churches built in Argyll in the late eighteenth century (see also Kilmodan, above). It was built between 1787 and 1791 to designs by Thomas Cairns. It is beautifully proportioned, and its intrinsic architectural quality is complemented by its setting on the west coast of the Kintyre peninsula. The purity of its design has been slightly compromised by the addition of a belfry in 1879, by Robert Weir. The interior is relatively little altered, with a canopied pulpit, box pews and a horseshoe gallery. Of the other Argyll neoclassical churches, Kilmodan is also good, but is not so well proportioned. The church replaced a medieval building on a different site, the ruins of which still survive. The rebuilding of Argyll churches at this period reflects the improvement of the agriculture in the area, and possibly the success of the illicit distilling industry, which supplied the Glasgow market for good-quality whisky.

71. *St Magnus' Parish Church, Tingwall*

The least altered of the late eighteenth-century churches in Shetland, this is a plain, rectangular, harled building of 1788–90, with an unusual round-headed belfry. Internally, there is a gallery round three sides, supported on cast-iron columns, and with plain, panelled fronts. The pulpit has a square base and an octagonal upper section, with columns on the front angles supporting the square top. The sounding board is of a type peculiar to Shetland, with an ogival canopy, with radial panelling on the underside (see also Lunnasting, above). The Tingwall building replaced one of three medieval churches in Shetland which had, like Egilsay in Orkney, western round towers. Behind the eighteenth-century building is the burial vault of the Mitchells of Westshore (an earlier name for Scalloway). This is now turf-covered, like an icehouse, but has a round-headed, roll-moulded doorway. Among the persons buried in the aisle is Andrew Crawford, Master of Works to the Earl of Orkney, who was responsible for the construction of the Earl's Palace in Kirkwall and Scalloway Castle.

72. *Annan Old Parish Church*

*B*uilt of the rich red sandstone of southern Dumfriesshire, Annan Old is a more modest version of such churches as the High Kirk, Paisley and Irvine Old. Unlike them, it is constructed on a level site and on the main road through the town – less dramatic, but more a part of the streetscape of the town. When the church was built, Annan was a busy port on the Solway, with a rich agricultural hinterland. The body of the church was completed in 1789–90, with a projecting tower, and the steeple was added to the tower in 1798–1801. It was probably part of the original design. The canopied magistrates' pew in the north gallery, installed when the church was built, survives, but the columns supporting the galleries were replaced in 1873–4, when the church was refurnished and a session house built on to the north side, to designs by Hugh Ker. On the east side of the churchyard is a statue of Edward Irving (1792–1834), a native of Annan and a gifted preacher whose followers in London eventually founded the Catholic Apostolic Church. This monument is by J. W. Dods, and was constructed in 1871–2.

73. *Montrose Old and St Andrew's Parish Church*

*L*ike so many of the eighteenth-century churches so far described, Montrose Old was built for a successful port. The body of the church, designed by John Gibson and built in 1791–3, is distinguished in having two tiers of galleries, a rare feature. It also has pointed windows, a very early example of the 'Gothick' in Scotland. These were retraceried in about 1860. It is the extraordinary steeple that justifies its inclusion here. It is a larger version of that at St Mungo's, Alloa, and like it was designed by James Gillespie Graham. Both are based on the steeple of Louth Parish Church, Lincolnshire. The Montrose steeple is the most prominent feature of the town centre and may well have been intended to be a navigational aid, for it is clearly visible from the sea. The interior was remodelled in 1883, when an apse was added on the south side. The galleries are supported on Roman-Doric columns. The pulpit and organ case are modern. The church contains a brass chandelier of 1623, of Dutch origin.

74. *Catrine Parish Church*

*T*his was probably the first church in Scotland designed specifically to serve an industrial community. The village of Catrine was laid out to house workers in a large, water-powered, cotton-spinning mill built from 1787 by David Dale, a Glasgow entrepreneur, and local landowner Sir Claud Alexander of Ballochmyle, who had made a fortune in India. The church was built in 1792 as a chapel of ease of the parish of Sorn, and sits on a south-facing slope above the site of the mills and of the housing, some of which survives. The design of the church is very advanced for the time, in a fully-blown 'Gothick' style. The large pointed windows have Y-tracery and intersecting-arc glazing. This gives the whole an impression of lightness and elegance unmatched in any other Scottish church of the period. It was renovated in 1874, and again in 1960 and subsequently.

75. *St Fergus' Parish Church, Glamis*

*T*his church, dating from 1792, is on a very old Christian site, as shown by a fine Pictish sculptured slab in the manse garden, opposite the church. It replaced a church of 1242. This is a transitional building, with a simple classical steeple at the west end, and a 'Gothick' body, with pointed windows and Y-tracery in what was originally a horse-shoe-galleried, rectangular interior, with the pulpit on the long wall. To the east is the late-medieval Strathmore Aisle, built in 1459 as a burial aisle by Isabella Ogilvy for the burial of her husband, Patrick Lyon, First Lord Glamis. It is barrel-vaulted with heraldic sculpture, and is now used as a small hall. A fine, modern, stained-glass window in the south gable of the aisle commemorates the seventeenth Earl of Strathmore and the wedding of his daughter in 1993. The interior of the body of the church was remodelled in 1933 in Ecclesiological Movement manner, with the pulpit, Communion table and font at the east end in a new, broad chancel. There is a broad gallery at the west end, with a Gothic-panelled front carved by the men of the parish under the direction of a local art teacher. The effect is remarkable: a clean, open, early twentieth-century interior making no reference to the eighteenth-century exterior.

76. *Glenaray and Inveraray Parish Church, Inveraray*

*T*his church, built in 1792, is the earliest example in Scotland of a church designed for the centre of a regularly-planned settlement. It was an integral part of the Duke of Argyll's new town of Inveraray, which replaced a straggling village further up Loch Fyne that interfered with the setting of the Duke's residence, Inveraray Castle. Because Gaelic was still widely spoken in the area, there were two worship spaces within the symmetrical building: the northern (Glenaray) one for Gaelic speakers, and the southern (Inveraray) one for the English-speaking congregation. The design, by Robert Mylne, is also unusual in that the pedimented ends have free-standing columns at the corners, and pilasters in the centre. There was originally a central slender steeple (fleche), but this was taken down during the Second World War. The Gaelic church was converted into the church hall in 1957. The rear gallery is original, and the side galleries were added in 1898–9, when the church was remodelled by Charles and Edward MacLaren, with an open-timber, king-post roof. They designed the large pulpit, supported on six tall columns and based on one in the baptistery of Pisa Cathedral, and an elaborate timber reredos, with Gothic tracery and a crested canopy. This has been painted grey, probably by Ian G. Lindsay and Partners, who renovated the town in the 1950s. Inveraray remains the outstanding example of an Enlightenment planned town, and the church contributes very significantly to its rational dignity.

77. Baldernock Parish Church

A delightful small church built in 1795, on the site of a thirteenth-century building, to serve an agricultural parish. Its layout is typical for a country church of the period, arranged primarily for preaching, with the pulpit in the middle of the long south wall, and galleries on the other three sides. The galleries are approached by external stairs on the east and west walls, a rare feature by that time. Externally, the architectural emphasis is on the south front, with the belfry above an advanced and pedimented central feature, flanked by tall round-headed windows with intersecting-arc glazing. Below the pediment is an incised inscription in Latin, which may be translated 'To God the best and greatest! To the Father, the Son and the Holy Ghost. 1795.' In the graveyard is a watch-house dated 1828, used to deter body snatchers.

78. Bellie Parish Church, Fochabers

T his church was designed as the central feature of the fourth Duke of Gordon's planned village of Fochabers. Like Inveraray, the village replaced an earlier, irregular one – in this case, in the grounds of Gordon Castle – with its own parish church. The church, completed in 1798 to designs by John Baxter junior, has an orthodox, simple classical steeple, but the frontage is a Greek-Doric portico, the first such in Scotland. There is a semicircular apse on the south wall, originally filled with curved pews. The building has twice been radically remodelled internally, first by Archibald Simpson in the 1830s, when the layout was reversed and Greek detailing applied. In the second reordering, in 1954, the original orientation was restored, by George Bennett Mitchell and Son, Aberdeen. The pulpit, though altered, retains part of its 1798 fabric. The Greek Revival Communion table and font date from 1931. Three stained-glass windows by Shona McInnes were installed in the apse to mark the bicentenary of the building. This is a remarkable building for its location, a reminder of the taste and aspirations of the fourth Duke.

79. *Highland Parish Church, Campbeltown*

*T*his building was constructed in 1803 to a design by George Dempster of Greenock, as a church for Gaelic speakers to complement the Lowland Church (now converted into flats). It is on a T-plan, at the top of a hill. The façade treatment is unusual, with the centre and ends advanced from the rest of the body of the building. The lack of a clear central emphasis, apart from the tower, is slightly unsettling. It was originally designed with a belfry, but the heritors insisted on a steeple, and one was built in 1836. It was twice struck by lightning, but was rebuilt on both occasions, most recently in 1884 when the interior was remodelled, with a horse-shoe gallery supported on cast-iron columns and a semi-octagonal pulpit. The interior was again reordered in a more limited way in 1954–5. It appears to be the only church in southern Scotland built specifically for a Gaelic-speaking congregation which is still in use for worship. At the time of its construction Gaelic was still widely spoken in Argyll, but the planned town of Campbeltown had also attracted settlers from the English-speaking Lowlands.

80. *Echt Parish Church*

*L*ike Catrine, this is a 'Gothick' building, but architecturally it is less obviously accomplished, though no less attractive. It was designed by William and Andrew Clerk and built in 1804. The vernacular quality, combined with the pointed windows with intersecting-arc tracery, gives this building immediate and lasting appeal, only marred by a mid-twentieth-century clock face in the gabled front. Inside it is the original gallery, but the wooden ceiling (based on the ceiling in St Machar's Cathedral, Aberdeen – see above) and chancel fittings date from 1930 and were designed by William Kelly. The church and adjacent village of Echt served the Dunecht Estate, bought in the early twentieth century by a rich civil engineering contractor, Lord Cowdray, who probably paid for the remodelling in 1930.

81. *Saltoun Parish Church, East Saltoun*

*S*altoun was built in 1805 on the site of an earlier building, for John Fletcher Campbell 'as a monument to the virtues of the ancestors'. It was probably designed by Robert Brown. Like Echt, Saltoun is less than architecturally correct, but for me, at least, it has a powerful appeal. It is in a style all its own, with an unusually slender spire rising from a squat battlemented tower. The T-plan body of the church has small three-light windows, and the roof is also set behind a parapet, an early example of this arrangement in a Scots church. Internally, the church is calm and spacious to an unusual degree. It was refurnished in 1885, probably by John Lessels. Its appeal is enhanced by the reddish East Lothian sandstone of which it is built, and by the varied greens of its woodland setting.

82. *Bourtie Parish Church*

*T*his is a tiny church for a small rural parish. It was probably designed by W. and A. Clerk, the architects of Echt Parish Church (see above), and built in 1806. It has a steeply-pitched, piended (hipped) roof over a broad, rectangular worship space lit by two tall 'Gothick' windows on the south front and similarly-glazed fanlights above the two doorways on the north front. There is a minute, ogee-headed, ball-finialled belfry on the west wall-head. Internally, the church is virtually unaltered, with a horse-shoe gallery, box pews and an elegant canopied pulpit. Despite not being great architecture, this is a singularly pleasing little kirk, eminently fit for purpose and powerfully evocative of the rural Aberdeenshire of two centuries ago, when agricultural improvement had not yet depopulated the countryside, and when the French Wars had raised the prices of all agricultural products.

83. *St Michael's Parish Church, Inveresk*

*B*uilt on the site of a sixth-century church, this is a late and fine example of a large burgh church with a classical steeple. Designed by Robert Nisbet and built in 1806, it is on an elevated site in the high-class suburb of Inveresk, and is approached by a steep, broad flight of stairs from a wide gateway, giving enhanced scale and presence to an already exceptionally-large building. The steeple is well proportioned and detailed, as is the entrance, but the overall effect is reduced by the use of segment-headed windows, which are less effective than either rectangular or round-headed windows in buildings of this type. Nonetheless, this is a powerful building. Internally, as in Montrose Old (see above) and the Barclay Church, Edinburgh (see below), there are two tiers of galleries, the upper one for the fisherfolk of Fisherrow, a suburb of Musselburgh. The interior was remodelled in 1893 to designs by J. MacIntyre Henry.

84. *Peterhead Old Parish Church*

*T*his is another large, classical-steepled burgh church, for the fishing port of Peterhead, in north-east Aberdeenshire, but it is very different in character to other examples of the type. It was constructed in 1804–6, and designed by Alexander Laing, a local architect, with some input from Robert Mitchell of Edinburgh, as insisted by the heritors, who lived in Edinburgh. The body of the church is low, almost squat, with a piended roof, and the spire is tall and slender. This sounds an awkward combination, but in fact it gives the spire both a satisfactory, solid base and a soaring quality otherwise found only in St Luke's, Greenock (below) in churches of this type. Internally, there is a U-plan gallery with finely-panelled fronts, supported on reeded Roman-Doric columns. The rest of the interior was remodelled in 1894, and restored in 1966, when the present pulpit was installed. The main interest of the building lies in its exterior which is a notable contribution to the character of the town.

85. St George's Tron Parish Church, Glasgow

*B*eginning a move away from what might be described as Georgian classicism as the preferred style for large urban churches, this building can only be described as baroque. Its architect, William Stark, did not build many buildings, but all are original – and most are powerful – compositions. Constructed in 1807, this is the largest of his three churches (see also Muirkirk, below). It is set on an island site, looking east towards George Square, in what used to be called St George's Square, renamed Nelson Mandela Square in the 1970s by the city council. The five obelisk-shaped finials on the building were intended to be statues: one can only be thankful that there was not the money to execute this fussy intention. Internally, the building has been much altered, on several occasions, but retains its horse-shoe gallery and a circular pulpit of 1851 on an octagonal column. The pulpit has a low-relief, arcaded frieze round it, and there are similarly-detailed motifs on the gallery fronts, above each of the slender, cast-iron columns. The flat ceiling has an enormous ceiling rose, probably installed to support and ventilate a sizeable gasolier. The east front is definitely the show front; the west front, with a low vestry block, is an anti-climax, though the distant view of the building from the top of West George Street is sufficiently impressive. The building now suffers from the clutter of road signs that are an inevitable result of modern systems of managing road and pedestrian traffic, but its design is sufficiently powerful to overcome such distractions.

86. Glenorchy Parish Church, Dalmally

A late example of the octagonal churches which came into favour in the late eighteenth century, Glenorchy, designed by James Elliot for the Earl of Breadalbane in 1808 and completed in 1811, can also be considered one of the first true Gothic revival (rather than Gothick) churches in Scotland. It is not particularly large, but as it is set on a knoll it is one of the most striking churches in the west Highlands. This is the third church on this site, which appears to have been in use for worship at least since the early medieval period. The pyramid-roofed octagon has buttresses at the corners, extended above the wall-head and terminating in obelisks, with a single large pointed window on each side, apart from the east face, which abuts the chunky bell tower. The tower pinnacles have similar detailing to the buttresses on the body of the church. The tracery of all but one of the windows was replaced in metal in 1898, when the building was refurbished by Kenneth Macrae of Oban. Internally, there is a U-plan gallery with panelled front. The pulpit, below the west window, dates from the 1898 renovations. The building is harled, with exposed masonry dressings, an unusual treatment for a Gothic building.

87. *Muirkirk Parish Church*

*T*his is one of two smaller churches designed by William Stark in a thoroughly original manner (see also St George's Tron, Glasgow, above). At the time of the construction of this church in 1812, Muirkirk was one of a handful of important Scottish iron-working towns, with ironstone and coal pits to service the blast furnaces. The chunky aesthetic suits the grittiness of the grimy place Muirkirk must have been. The window frames appear to be of cast iron, and if so were presumably made in the ironworks. The building was burned out in the late 1940s, so all the present interior post-dates that event. As built, the arrangement of the windows indicates that it had a horse-shoe gallery. The layout, though not the detailing, of this church anticipates the 'Heritors' Gothic' buildings exemplified by Collace (see below). Muirkirk, despite its remote moorland location, has survived the loss both of its iron-working and of its coal-mining industries, and this church is important as the only building of any real quality in the village.

88. *Collace Parish Church, Kinrossie*

*A*pparently a typical parish church of the period, Collace, built in 1813, seems to have been the first of a generation of such churches, modelled on a generic English village church externally, but rather different internally, with a horse-shoe gallery and a central pulpit on the 'east' wall. The window tracery in such buildings is generally Perpendicular, and there is almost always a square bell (and clock) tower. Tower and buttresses are usually capped with pinnacles. James Gillespie Graham designed many of them, and probably designed this one. Collace replaced a Romanesque church of 1242,

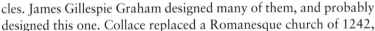

probably on account of the growing population of the area which had resulted from agricultural improvement and high prices for grain during the Napoleonic Wars. The church is built of the local pinkish sandstone, and is on a knoll. The quality of the detailing and the handling of the massing of the building is much more accomplished than in many later examples of the type. The interior was recast in 1908. When the old church was demolished, some of the masonry, including the chancel arch, was used to build the Nairne Mausoleum in the churchyard. The churchyard also contains an early nineteenth-century vaulted mort-house, used to keep corpses until they were of no use to anatomists at a time when the removal of corpses from fresh graves was a real threat. The church is adjacent to the Improvement village of Kinrossie.

89. *Nicolson Square Methodist Church, Edinburgh*

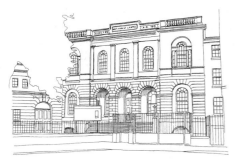

*V*ery much in keeping with Edinburgh taste of the period, this church resembles the recasing of the buildings in Parliament Square carried out at about the same time, and the Robert Adam design for the west front of Edinburgh University. The designer was Thomas Brown, and it was built in 1815–16. Internally, there is a contemporary U-plan gallery. The anachronistic pulpit was designed by Peter Macgregor Chalmers for Lady Glenorchy's Church in Roxburgh Place in 1913, and came here in 1974. Methodism was never particularly popular in Scotland, and its members often came from England.

90. *North Leith Parish Church, Edinburgh*

A late and fine large burgh church, built in 1816, with classical steeple and Greek-Doric portico, set to look down Prince Regent Street in the New Town of Leith. According to the *Buildings of Scotland: Edinburgh*, its design is based on that of the hall block at Downing College, Cambridge (1807–20), by William Wilkins, pioneer of the Greek revival in England. It is probably the best, architecturally, of that genre of churches, but its perfection is somewhat chilly, especially as it faces north. Internally, it has a horse-shoe gallery, in the manner of the time, supported on Doric columns, and a classical pulpit. This is not the original, which was supplanted by an organ in 1880, but a replacement of 1950, made by Scott Morton and Co. and installed during a refurbishment by Ian G. Lindsay and Partners. The layout is unusual in that the main entrances to the worship space are at the front, through doors flanking the pulpit. At the time of its construction Leith was a very prosperous port and manufacturing town, with an extensive trade with continental Europe and London. There is every reason to suppose that its leading citizens were both people of taste and aware of current architectural fashion south of the border.

91. *St Andrew's Catholic Cathedral, Glasgow*

This was the first large Catholic church built in Scotland after the Reformation, in 1816, and was designed to accommodate 2,000 people, at a time when Catholics were migrating into Glasgow from the Highlands and Ireland in considerable numbers, many of them to work in the city's cotton mills. It was intended as a statement of the confident return of Roman Catholicism to the city, and is an externally-elaborate structure in the newly-fashionable Gothic Revival style, which with its medieval links was especially appropriate for a Catholic church. With its crocketted finials, prominent buttresses and ogee-headed doorway, all in a fifteenth-century manner, it was by far the most elaborate Gothic Revival church built up to that time in Scotland. It was constructed on a restricted site, with its gable to the street, in what has been termed the 'English College Chapel' style. As with the English Parish Church layout introduced at Collace (above), this approach to church design became very popular, especially for churches squeezed into narrow-fronted urban building plots. The Roman Catholic hierarchy in Scotland was restored in 1878, creating the Archdiocese of Glasgow – an archdiocese because of the enormous size of the Catholic population, which had expanded dramatically as a consequence of Irish and Highland immigration. St Andrew's was made the cathedral in 1889, and was altered in 1889, 1897 and 1904 to suit that purpose. The architects were Pugin and Pugin. The construction of large numbers of Catholic churches elsewhere in the city, many of them also designed by Pugin and Pugin, reduced the pressure on St Andrew's, and the side galleries installed when the church was built were removed in 1904. The church has been re-ordered on several occasions since. Externally, it is largely as built, apart from the insertion of confessionals between the buttresses on the east side, and the removal of some of the pinnacles. The front outer and inner doors were designed by Gillespie, Kidd and Coia. Despite much building and rebuilding in the vicinity, the cathedral remains a very striking feature of the waterfront.

92. *St Andrew's Scottish Episcopal Church, Aberdeen*

*T*his is another example of an 'English College Chapel' church, sandwiched between contemporary three-storey tenements. It was built in 1817, and designed by Archibald Simpson, the leading Aberdeen architect of the period, as the centrepiece of King Street Terrace, first laid out in 1803. Its façade design is simpler than that of St Andrew's Roman Catholic Cathedral, Glasgow, with two tall, crocketted finials flanking the entrance. These stand above the neighbouring buildings in long views, signing the position of the church. Initially, the building was a plain rectangle in plan, but under the influence of the Oxford Movement a chancel was added in 1880 to designs by G. E. Street. The porch was added in 1911 by Sir Robert Lorimer, detracting from the original design intention, but for practical reasons. The interior was substantially remodelled between 1936 and 1943 by Sir Ninian Comper, a notably-sensitive episcopalian architect. The effect is striking, with the emblems of the United States of America emblazoned on the white-painted, plaster, vaulted ceiling. This is an allusion to the fact that the first bishop of the Anglican communion in the United States was ordained by the then Bishop of Aberdeen.

93. *Channelkirk Parish Church*

*P*robably James Gillespie Graham's most modest church, this was a remarkably fashionable church for a remote country parish. Its sophistication was probably due to the influence of the principal heritor, the Earl of Lauderdale. It was built in 1817 to replace an earlier church on this site, and is on a T-plan, with Gothick windows and crenellated gables. The belfry has a crocketted top and arched openings. Internally, the church retains its original pulpit and box pews, which are painted and grained. It is in a remote upland area in Berwickshire, set among rolling hills, and its environs can have changed little since it was built.

94. *St Mungo's Parish Church, Alloa*

*T*he Gothic Revival crocketted and finialled church reached its
Scottish apogee in St Mungo's, Alloa (1817–19) and St John's
Episcopal, Edinburgh (below). St Mungo's is, in essence, a large
Scots T-plan burgh church, but it is dressed up with the full panoply
of late Gothic trimmings, including a tall steeple (207 feet high) with
diagonal flying buttresses, modelled on that of Louth, Lincolnshire,
set in the middle of its street frontage. Like the similar but taller
steeple of Montrose Old, this was probably intended in part as a
navigational aid, as Alloa was a prosperous port when the church
was built, importing timber and grain and exporting coal and beer.
The building was designed by James Gillespie Graham, and externally can be considered his masterpiece. Additions were made on
both east and west gables in the early twentieth century by Leslie
Grahame MacDougall. The interior has been much altered, and is
not very appealing.

95. *St John the Evangelist's Scottish Episcopal Church, Edinburgh*

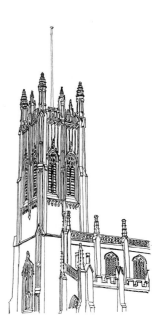

*I*n essence this is an enlarged version of Collace, but it is much
more elaborate externally, and the nave is aisled. It was designed
by William Burn, and was originally built in 1818 on a rectangular
plan, with a U-plan gallery and a central pulpit. The tower, on the
west end, originally terminated in an octagonal lantern, but this collapsed during construction, and was replaced by the present, more
conventional arrangement. When completed, it must have formed a
startling contrast to the late eighteenth-century classical St
Cuthbert's parish church in the valley below, and indeed to the deep-
rooted classicism of Edinburgh at the time, when the city was
known as the 'Athens of the North' and tried very hard to build on
that reputation. The explicitly English character of St John's is
strongly reinforced in its interior, with its plaster fan-vaulted ceiling,
modelled on such buildings as King's College Chapel, Cambridge.
In 1867 Peddie and Kinnear removed the galleries on either side of
the altar, and refitted the church with a new pulpit, pews and panelling on the aisle walls. In 1879–82 they built a chancel with an
apsidal end over what was originally a burial enclosure. The present
Gothic reredos was installed in 1889 by Kinnear and Peddie. The
last major alteration to the interior was in 1913, when the west

gallery was taken back into the tower. The stained glass is of considerable interest, and because of the size of the windows the interior remains bright and welcoming. In its present form, the church is architecturally convincing both inside and out. Its position on one of the busiest corners in Edinburgh makes it difficult to view the exterior to advantage, but it is well worth taking the trouble to look seriously at it.

96. *Kirk o'Shotts (Shotts Parish Church)*

One of the most strikingly situated parish churches in Scotland, and now a notable landmark on the M8 motorway between Glasgow and Edinburgh, Kirk o'Shotts is another Gillespie Graham church, built in 1820 to serve a large, mainly rural, upland parish. The only large settlement in the parish was Shotts village, whose iron-smelting works was one of the largest in Scotland (and which supplied much of the iron to make the railings, window-guards and other ornamental ironwork for the later phases of the New Town of Edinburgh). The rural setting of the church is presumably because the local landowners wished it to be convenient for them rather than for the iron-workers and the miners in the pits which supplied the works. Though the church has neither tower nor spire, it is a spacious one, and with its galleried interior could accommodate large numbers of worshippers. The interior is largely unaltered, and gives a wonderful impression of what one of the first generation of Gothic Revival churches was like. There is a very real sense in this church of the generations of parishioners who met in this bleak setting to worship their Lord. This was Covenanting country, and its people took their faith seriously.

97. Dunfermline Abbey Church

*T*his is another Gillespie Graham building, this time in 'Village Church' mode, but on an unusually-large scale and cruciform, a rarity in a church of this period and character. It replaced in 1818–21 the ruins of the thirteenth-century choir, transepts and crossing of the abbey church, abandoned after the Reformation (see Dunfermline Abbey above). Its most distinctive feature is the incorporation in the parapet of the tower of the words 'KING ROBERT THE BRUCE', reflecting the fact that the Bruce's tomb is in the church, under the  pulpit. Beside the vigour of the Romanesque nave of the Abbey and its massive, later buttresses (see above), Gillespie Graham's design looks weaker than it actually is. Internally, the unusual height of the building is evident. The height was necessary to give the building a significant presence beside the Abbey nave. The ceiling is plaster-vaulted, in a rather thin and unconvincing manner. The choir was refurnished in 1890 by Sir R. Rowand Anderson, who was also responsible for the present scheme of decoration, executed in 1905. On the north wall of the north transept is the Magistrates' Pew of 1610. There is something vaguely unsatisfying about the worship space, hardly redeemed by some good twentieth-century stained glass, but the building sits well in its graveyard setting.

98. Broughton St Mary's (St Mary's) Parish Church, Edinburgh

*M*ore typical of early nineteenth-century Edinburgh than St John's Episcopal Church (above), St Mary's is one of a number of new parish churches built to serve the expanding city. It was con-structed for the town council in 1824, and designed by Thomas Brown, City Superintendent of Works. The scale and elaboration of this church reflects the relatively-wealthy area it was designed to serve, but it was probably also intended to rival the newly-built United Secession Greek-Doric church a short distance away in Broughton Place. St Mary's is the centrepiece of Bellevue Crescent, and is also on the axis of East Claremont Street, a broad approach to the northern New Town. This use of church buildings as centre-pieces and visual stops has been mentioned under Inveraray, Bellie and St George's Tron (above), and was particularly in vogue in

Edinburgh, a city in the vanguard of formal town planning in the late eighteenth and early nineteenth centuries. St Mary's is worthy of its setting. It has the classical portico (in this case Corinthian rather than the more usual Doric) that was part of the standard architectural vocabulary of the time, but instead of a steeple there is a tall cupola, an effective and striking innovation. Internally, the church has a rounded east end (back), a U-plan gallery, and an unobstructed neo-Greek ceiling. The building was altered in 1874 by John Lessels, who formed a platform at the front of the worship space and lowered the pulpit, removing the precentor's box which sat at the base of the structure. The pulpit is exceptionally fine, with a cylindrical body supported on a column and approached on both sides by stairs with elegant iron balustrades. The sounding board is also circular, supported on a pair of columns and surmounted by a reeded dome. The pews date from 1897 and were designed by Sydney Mitchell. The classical font was made in 1904. The stained glass is of good quality. Altogether the church remains remarkably unaltered, and still fulfils its original intention of being a fine piece of townscape as well as an effective place of worship.

99. Ettrick Parish Church

*T*here are few churches in Scotland more isolated than Ettrick, in remotest Selkirkshire, the most sparsely-populated county in southern Scotland. The parish it serves is an upland, sheep-farming one, and this is not a place for architectural niceties. The massing is that of a Gothic Revival 'Village Church', but it is more uncompromising than that, with a battlemented tower and rectangular windows with Tudor-style hoodmoulds. It was built in 1824 to replace a church of 1619, a memorial stone from which is built into the south wall of the new structure. Internally, it is galleried, implying that its parish was more densely populated then than now, and it is little altered, with its original laird's loft and pulpit. James Hogg (1770–1845), the poet known as the Ettrick Shepherd, is buried in the graveyard. As with all churches in remote areas, the building is affecting because of the way it embodies the role of a territorial church in the lives of a scattered population.

100. Lecropt Parish Church

*T*hough conforming in most respects – externally, at least – to the formulaic 'Heritors' Gothic' or English Village Church pattern, this building is significantly more elegant and refined than the generality of such buildings. Built on a striking site overlooking the low-lying Carse of Stirling, it was designed by William Stirling, of the family of the Stirlings of Keir, and built in 1826 as the estate church. It is built of a white sandstone, which has weathered to a light grey and shows up well against its wooded setting. The elegant interior is in Tudor Gothic style, with the nave spanned by a four-centred arched and ribbed ceiling. The shallow chancel has a plaster-groined vaulted ceiling. The Keir loft is at the tower end of the church, and originally had a private access up the tower. It is lower than usual in such features, and is divided into three compartments by clustered columns, supporting plaster-groined sub-vaults. On the rear wall there are memorials to members of the Stirling family. The pulpit is original.

101. Limekilns Parish Church

*I*n the mid-eighteenth century several groups split (seceded) from the established Church of Scotland on the issue of the right of landowners to appoint ministers, and the largest of these groups split in turn in a manner far too complex to describe here (see Introduction). In 1820 most of the Secession congregations reunited as the United Secession Church. This body built a number of new churches, all classical, and most of them with pilastered and pedimented fronts – 'flat classical' – as opposed to porticos with columns in the round. Limekilns (1825–6) is a good example of a 'flat classical' United Secession church and, unlike most, it is still in use. Secession churches did not have bells, but a belfry was added to the rear gable here in 1911, by Hippolyte J. Blanc. Internally the building has a U-plan gallery. The Jacobean pulpit dates from 1883. This church was built to serve an area where there was coal-mining. Limekilns was itself a minor port on the Forth, and its two piers can still be seen.

102. Croick Parish Church

*E*xpansion of population in early nineteenth-century Scotland was by no means confined to the towns and villages, and in the northern and western Highlands this left large areas without adequate church accommodation. Successive governments had invested substantially in Highland roads and bridges, in harbours and in the Caledonian Canal, largely with the intention of retaining population in the area. In the late 1820s the government decided to carve 'Parliamentary Parishes' out of the large, old-established civil and religious parishes, and to provide them with simple churches and manses. These were built under the auspices of Thomas Telford, who was building the Highland roads at the time, but the designer was William Thomson. Externally, they were simple, dignified structures. The front elevations of the churches had two large central windows, with Y-tracery and diamond-pane glazing in cast-iron frames, and flanking doorways with fanlights. All the openings have four-centred arched heads, giving a mildly Tudor feel to the design. Croick, built in 1827, is a notably unaltered example, with its original internal layout and furnishings, including a long Communion table running across the church in front of the pulpit, round which the communicants gathered in relays to receive the sacrament. The original Parliamentary manse also survives here. This church would be worth including in this book for that reason alone, but it is particularly famous for its involvement in the notorious 'Clearances', when it was used as a gathering place for families being forcibly removed from Glen Calvie in 1845 to make way for the less labour-intensive rearing of sheep. The distress this caused is recorded as scratched messages on the windows of the church. There is an extraordinary immediacy about the impact of being in the worship space in this church, hinting not just at the depopulation of the area, but also at the extent of population growth that preceded the Clearances.

103. Cortachy Parish Church

*S*ituated in one of the glens which stretch north and west from lowland Angus, Cortachy is an estate church, built in 1828 for the seventh Earl of Airlie, who lived nearby at Cortachy Castle. It replaced an earlier building on this site, and is a small rectangular building. Externally, it is an elaborate exercise in early Gothic Revival style, with Perpendicular windows of much more sophisticated design than normal in such buildings. Internally, it is galleried, and contains memorials to the ninth and twelfth earls. The burial aisle of the Airlie family is on the east gable of the building, looking from the outside like a chancel. This is a very surprising building to find in such a remote rural place, but an altogether delightful one.

104. St Stephen's Church Centre, Edinburgh

*L*ike St Mary's Broughton, St Stephen's, completed in 1828, is one of the new parish churches built by the town council to serve the expanding city of Edinburgh. Unlike St Mary's, however, it is a seriously innovative, if unique, one. The building was originally intended to be on the west side of Royal Circus, looking along Great King Street, the principal street of the northern New Town laid out in 1801–2. In 1822 the present site was acquired, a difficult one. The designer of St Stephen's, William H. Playfair, took advantage of the steeply-sloping site to have the entrance to the worship space at gallery level, through a monumental arch at the head of a broad flight of steps flanked by extraordinary scrolled features on a gigantic scale. As if this was not unusual enough, the building is square on plan, but set on a diagonal, with the entrance and distinctively-detailed tower on the south-facing corner. The church is at the bottom of St Vincent Street, to which it forms a very effective visual stop. It defines the transition from the main body of the second New Town to less formally-planned streets, and to the industrial area of Silvermills (now being developed residentially). The massively-tall, plain, octagonal worship space, never acoustically satisfactory, was divided horizontally at gallery level in 1955 by Gilbert H. Jenkins of London in one of the first such conversions, keeping the gallery pews, and moving the gallery fronts to the rear walls. The classical pulpit, designed by David Rhind and installed in 1880, was raised to the new level. The lower part of the building was retained as a hall. The building is no longer used for regular worship, but is still used for church purposes, and as a performance space during the Edinburgh Festival. This extraordinary building works externally at a number of levels, even though it was never satisfactory as a church. Looking down the steeply-sloping Howe Street and St Vincent Street, its tower is seen against a background of the Firth of Forth and the hills of Fife. From a nearer viewpoint one loses consciousness of its larger setting, and the converging tenements on either side focus attention on the masterly massing of the building and on its sparing but effective detailing. Close up, the vast scale of the structure becomes apparent, with the lavish spaciousness delivered by the giant scrolled features flanking the stairs being the dominant, Baroque effect. This is one of the few churches in Scotland that can truly be described as magnificent.

105. *St Giles' Parish Church, Elgin*

*B*ellie, North Leith and St Mary's Broughton have already been introduced as early Greek revival churches (above), but St Giles, Elgin, constructed between 1825 and 1828, is in a different league in terms of the inventive use of Greek classical motifs. Like Inveraray and St George's Tron, Glasgow, it is a central feature in a main street, but unlike them it is not in an 'Enlightenment' planned street setting; rather, it is in the middle of a medieval burgh market place, replacing an ancient church – the 'Muckle Kirk' – on the same site. It is thus not in a position to borrow dignity and regularity from its setting, but has to claim these by the strength of its design. This it does in a masterly way. Like the church at Inveraray, it looks both ways, but unlike it, the two principal frontages are very different in character. The main frontage faces west, and has a very well-detailed Doric portico rising, properly, from a stepped plinth. The other end is pilastered, and less correctly Greek, but the architect has managed to imbue this frontage with a genuinely Greek-classical feeling. Above this, but clearly visible from the other end, is what is in effect a steeple, but in this case is a version of the monument of Lysicrates, a popular neo-Greek motif. Set on top of the pilastered front, it gives that elevation a strength and articulation it would otherwise lack. Its real genius is, however, the way in which it gives life to the whole composition. As one moves along the street the 'steeple' is an eye-catcher, but not a dominant one, leading one to the portico and disappearing from sight at the point where the quality of the latter demands attention. This is a truly masterly building. It is only unfortunate that well-intentioned 'streetscape improvements', introduced when the thoroughfare was pedestrianised in the 1980s, have softened the setting, drawing the eye away from the compelling dynamic quality of this exceptional building. Internally, the building is disappointing. There is a good classical pulpit, and some other classical detailing, but there is no visual coherence to the interior as it currently exists. The pulpit came from the former Newington Parish Church in Edinburgh in 1981, when that building was converted into a concert hall. The interior demands the attention of either a modern classicist, or else a classical modernist to make it worthy of the exterior.

106. St Serf's Parish Church, Tillicoultry

*P*innacles have already been mentioned as characteristic, but not dominant, features of true Gothic Revival buildings, such as Collace, the St Andrew's cathedrals in Glasgow and Aberdeen, and St Mungo's, Alloa. In St Serf's, the parish church of Tillicoultry, opened in 1828, the pinnacles are the dominant feature, giving the building a unique character. It is not so much that they are particularly numerous, but rather that they are very large in relation to the mass of the building, and that the roof of the building is low-pitched, which gives them greater prominence than usual. This was advanced, but not great, architecture, and one must be grateful that its example was not copied. However, it is, in its own way, a remarkably pleasing structure. Unfortunately, tree growth is rapidly obscuring its qualities. The interior was remodelled in 1920, and is not of particular interest. Tillicoultry was already, when this church was built, noted for its woollen manufacture, as were the neighbouring towns of Alva and Alloa.

107. Portmoak Parish Church

*T*his church, built in 1832, is included as a good example of a type of church which was common in the first half of the nineteenth century, and which has not so far been noticed. This is essentially a larger version of Bourtie (see above), rectangular in plan, with a horse-shoe gallery. The pulpit is on the south long wall, and is flanked by tall windows. To the sides of this frontage there are pairs of windows, one lighting the gallery, and the other the ground floor below the gallery. Portmoak is a good, relatively-unaltered example of the type, and is chosen to represent it because of its magnificent situation on a south-facing slope with a wide prospect, and also in order to include a church from the small, mainly rural county of Kinross. In the churchyard are some good sculptured eighteenth-century headstones, and a monument to Michael Bruce, in the form of a sarcophagus on a stepped base. This monument was erected in 1842 to mark the burial place of the poet, who died in 1767 and who composed some of the paraphrases of passages of Scripture which were for generations sung as part of Reformed worship in Scotland.

108. Bothwell Parish Church

*T*he oldest part of this church is the choir of the collegiate church of St Bride, founded in 1398 by Archibald the Grim, Earl of Douglas, owner of Bothwell Castle. The collegiate church was added to the existing parish church. It is a heavily-buttressed rectangular building with a stone-slab roof, and has a sacristy attached to its north side. After the Reformation it seems to have been used as a mortuary chapel. It contains, among other memorials, a splendidly-elaborate marble monument to the second Duke of Hamilton, who died in 1694, which was transferred from the collegiate church of Hamilton in 1854. A new parish church was built in 1833 abutting the choir, on the site of the nave. It is in James Gillespie Graham's best 'Heritors' Gothic' style, buttresses, pinnacles, Perpendicular tracery and all. What makes the church distinguished among the many of this general character is the tower, at the junction between the new and the old, and on a scale which gives it genuine drama. At the time the extensive parish of Bothwell was largely agricultural. When it was built, the choir remained walled off. The two were united in 1933 in a complex project designed by J. Jeffrey Waddell, the leading Scots restoration architect of the period. The gallery in the 1833 building was removed, and the space thus created is not wholly successful, not helped by the removal of plaster from the interior of the choir. A prominent feature of the grounds of the building is a richly-decorated terracotta monument to Joanna Baillie, a poet and playwright well regarded in her day She was born in 1762, daughter of the minister of Bothwell, but from the age of fourteen until her death in 1851 lived in Hampstead, where she is buried. The monument, probably made by Doulton and Co., was commissioned by James Donald, and installed in 1899. The mosaic panels were made by the Murano Glass Co. Bothwell, though surrounded by what were industrial settlements, itself escaped industrialisation, and has since the mid-nineteenth century been a residential area.

109. Gordon Scottish Episcopal Chapel, Fochabers

*T*he parish church of Bellie, with its portico and classical steeple, is, as stated above, the centrepiece of the Duke of Gordon's planned village of Fochabers. The Gordon Chapel, opened in 1834, is also a set-piece, placed at the end of a street running north-south, and facing south. It was designed by Archibald Simpson of Aberdeen. Its simple but strikingly-dignified 'College Chapel' front is taller than usual in such churches, as the building is of two storeys, incorporating a school on the ground floor (now the rectory) with the worship space on the first floor. It was substantially remodelled in 1874. Apart from the show front, the main glory of the building is its fine stained glass by Morris and Co., some of the windows having been designed by Sir Edward Burne-Jones. The hammer-beam roof dates from the 1874 refurbishment, as do the furnishings. There are elegant late nineteenth-century brackets for oil lamps. Altogether, this is a delightful small episcopal church in the finest planned village in north-east Scotland.

110. St Margaret's Catholic Church, Huntly

*T*his was built in 1834 for a congregation of Scots 'Old Catholics', many of them descendants of people who had clung to the old religion at the Reformation. With worship in public now legal, the senior local clergyman, the Rt Rev. James Kyle, wanted to give the new church a distinctive architectural form, and this he achieved, with an octagonal worship space lit by lunette windows, and what can only be described as a baroque steeple. It was designed by the Rt Rev. James Kyle himself, possibly assisted by William Robertson. The effect is wonderful, with the top of the 'steeple' having a dynamic sculptural quality. The whole building has a lightness of touch which is a telling contrast to the Presbyterian places of worship in the town. St Thomas's, Keith is in something of the same style, but was never as architecturally accomplished, and lost much of its original character when it was enlarged in 1916 by C. J. Menart, a Belgian architect favoured by the Catholic Church in the early twentieth century. Internally, there are Spanish religious paintings beneath each of the lunettes, given by John Gordon of Wardhouse, and stencilled decoration. The altarpiece dates from 1902.

111. *St Mark's Unitarian Church, Edinburgh*

*T*his is the third of Scotland's great early nineteenth-century Baroque churches (with St George's Tron, Glasgow and St Margaret's, Huntly). It is, however, very different in character, being designed as a street-frontage building in a sinuous terrace of houses, part of Castle Terrace. Built between 1835 and 1836, as one of the early works of David Bryce, it sits well with the subdued classicism of its residential neighbours, but has an immediately exotic flavour deriving from its curvilinear, central wall-head feature, with pierced flanking parapets. The sophistication of the treatment of the façade, however, repays attention. The front windows have diamond-pane glazing, probably with zinc astragals. Internally, the worship space has an arched ceiling and a U-plan gallery. Only the sounding board of the Bryce pulpit survives.

112. *Ardchattan Parish Church, Achnaba*

*T*his large parish church is on a spectacular site on the north side of Loch Etive, and is a prominent feature in the landscape. At the time of its construction in 1836, it is probable that some worshippers came by boat. It has a gabled frontage with a louvred bellcote at the apex, a decent rather than accomplished piece of design. It is the interior that gives this church its special quality: an airy lightness reinforced by an elegant pulpit on a slender stem, and with a delicately-proportioned sounding board. Running along the centreline of the church is a long Communion table, one of the finest and longest in Scotland. To enter this church, particularly on a sunny day, is to have one's spirits lifted.

113. St Peter's Free Church, Dundee

One of the last churches in Scotland to be built with a classical steeple, St Peter's is set on a slope to the west of the city centre. It was built in 1835–6 as a chapel of ease at a time when the city's linen industry was expanding rapidly, to cope with the development of housing along the Perth Road, mainly for the burgeoning middle classes. The designers were the Hean Brothers, and the first minister was the Rev. Robert McCheyne (1813–43), a noted preacher, a pioneer of mission to the Jews, and one of the architects of the Disruption of 1843 (when the Free Church broke away from the Church of Scotland), though he died before it took place. St Peter's became a Free church in 1843, then United Free in 1900, and Church of Scotland in 1929. It became a Free church again in 1987. Internally, it has a horse-shoe gallery, supported on cast-iron columns. The organ and pulpit date from 1913. There are two good early twentieth-century stained-glass windows.

114. St Mary's Catholic Church, Inverness

Like a miniature version of St Andrew's Episcopal Cathedral in Aberdeen, and designed by William Robertson, St Mary's is one of the churches which line both sides of the river Ness in central Inverness. Its unaltered 'College Chapel' frontage of 1836–7 is linked by Gothic screen walls to flanking buildings, one of them the Presbytery. This façade gives a misleading impression of originality, however, for behind it the church has been completely rebuilt on a larger scale, in two stages. W. L. Carruthers extended it to the west in 1893, and in 1979 W. W. Allan added the south aisle and transept. The river frontage has a particular charm, bringing a gracefulness which is not found in any of the other seven churches on this stretch of river, despite their other merits.

115. *St Cuthbert's Parish Church, Kirkcudbright*

*A*t the end of the 1830s the first phase of the Gothic Revival in Scotland was virtually over, as was the vogue for classical steeples. Instead, steeples based, however loosely, on earlier medieval models came into vogue. St Cuthbert's was probably the first steepled Gothic Revival church in the country. It was designed by William Burn and built in 1835–8. In layout it is a large, but conventional T-plan building, with the down-stroke of the T, unusually, facing the street. Above the principal entrance is a well-proportioned and detailed steeple. The windows are simple lancets, with zinc lattice glazing. Internally, the church is spectacular, with three deep galleries (one of them with seats for the town council), original pews and a superb classical pulpit, perhaps the finest of its kind in Scotland. The setting is a striking one, as the building is in a large wooded graveyard in the very centre of the town, so that the church has a sense of repose, as well as being clearly in the heart of the community. The warm red sandstone of which it is built is set off in summer by the varied greens of its grounds.

116. *St Margaret's Catholic Church, Airdrie*

*T*his was the first Roman Catholic church built in north Lanarkshire since the Reformation. It was built in 1839, serving both the textile and mining burgh of Airdrie and the 'Iron Burgh' of Coatbridge. Both had immigrant Irish Catholic communities. Unusually for the period, the church was built in a 'flat classical' style, reflecting a wish for a 'modern' design. There is a simple classical steeple and the sides of the building have round-headed windows. Internally, the building is a plain rectangle. Originally there was a horse-shoe gallery, but the sides have been removed. There is a flat classical altarpiece, containing three mosaic panels relocated from a Glasgow church, though the altar is now advanced in post-Vatican II style. The walls and gallery front are decorated with small Rococo plaster details. The three-storey presbytery is on the west, and to the east is a building which was formerly the parish school. Despite alteration, the building is an affecting reminder of the early days of the restoration of Roman Catholicism in west central Scotland.

117. *Alyth Parish Church*

*A*t first glance this is a Gothic Revival church, but it has Romanesque detailing, and is one of a number of churches built in the late 1830s and 1840s in what may be termed the first Romanesque revival. The architects of these churches did not really understand the original buildings which provided patterns for their detailing, but the results are often engaging, as here at Alyth, constructed in 1839. The building was designed by Thomas Hamilton to replace the late fifteenth-century church of St Moluag, the remains of which still survive. Hamilton was also responsible for the free-standing arched porch at the entrance to the graveyard which surrounds the building. The massing of the building is similar to a number of other churches of the period, including Cambuslang Old and Barrhead Bourock. The interior was remodelled in 1934. There is a Pictish cross-slab in the porch which was found in the manse garden in 1887, and the church contains a hatchment (funerary representation of the arms) of Sir G. Ramsay of Bamff, dating from 1790–1.

118. *St Andrew's Parish Church (Gartsherrie Church), Coatbridge*

*T*he stimulus to the growth of Coatbridge was the iron-smelting industry, which grew rapidly in the 1830s after the invention of the hot-blast process. The leading firm was William Baird and Co., whose Gartsherrie Works lay to the north of the emerging town centre. In the late 1830s the Baird brothers bought up an area of ground between their works and the town centre, and laid it out for the building of middle-class housing. The site was on a hill, and on the summit of the hill they built this church, opened in 1839 and named after their works, looking down Baird Street towards Drumpellier House. The church, designed by Scott, Stephen and Gale, Glasgow, was the focal point of the development and was advanced architecturally, with the first Gothic Revival steeple north of Kirkcudbright, and geometric Gothic tracery in the side windows. The steeple, like a slender version of the spire of Glasgow Cathedral, is at the front of the building, and the body of the church is rectangular, with a horse-shoe gallery. The church and churchyard are surrounded by the original cast-iron railings.

119. *Penninghame St John's Parish Church, Newton Stewart*

Newton Stewart was founded in the seventeenth century. This is another early steepled Gothic Revival church, designed, like Kirkcudbright, by William Burn, and built between 1838 and 1840. Externally, the design has affinities with that of Gartsherrie, especially in the treatment of the lower part of the spire. The plan is, however, different, for Penninghame St John's is on a T-plan, with short 'transepts'. There is a ribbed, plaster-vaulted ceiling above a horse-shoe gallery. The Jacobean pulpit is part of Burn's original furnishings.

120. *St Luke's Parish Church (Old Church), Greenock*

Built in 1839–41 as a part of the development of the planned western 'new town' of Greenock, this church was designed by David Cousin, a versatile Glasgow architect who was also responsible, among others, for the Romanesque Cambuslang Old and the Gothic Revival Free High, Oban, churches. The congregation moved from the old West Church of 1591, which became a Gaelic church (see Old West Church, below). The church was intended to be a focal point at the end of Brisbane Street, and its tall body with its advanced and elevated central entrance bay was presumably meant to give it the necessary vertical emphasis. The design appears to have included a tall classical steeple, which was not, however, completed until 1855. The design of this feature can be traced back to one of Wren's City churches, but its most immediate ancestor was probably the steeple of Ayr Town Hall, designed by Thomas Hamilton and completed in 1832. The steeple of St Luke's, though strikingly elegant, does not have the exuberance of Hamilton's almost Rococo confection. The church was originally on a plain rectangular plan, but was remodelled in the 1912 by John Keppie with an apse to accommodate a large organ. It was completely refurnished at the same time.

121. *St Ninian's Scottish Episcopal Cathedral, Perth*

*T*his was the first cathedral built in Scotland since the Reformation, the earliest part being constructed in 1849–50 to designs by William Butterfield, a notable pioneer of the Gothic Revival in England. Its subsequent building history is exceptionally complex, so that unlike St Mary's Scottish Episcopal Cathedral, Edinburgh (see below), which is substantially of one period, St Ninian's is more medieval in character. By the time this building was started, Perth was an important centre of the dispersed local bleaching and dyeing trade, and a market town for the rich, improved farming area of the Tay, Almond and Earn valleys. The town was also becoming a focal point on the embryonic railway system of central Scotland. The first part of the church to be completed was the choir, crossing, transept and the start of the nave. Construction stalled there until 1888, when building to Butterfield's design was resumed. The nave was completed and a start made on a west tower before building again ended in 1890. Between 1901 and 1911 J. L. and F. L. Pearson revisited the whole concept, demolishing the partly-completed west tower and replacing it with a gabled front flanked by octagonal pinnacles, and remodelling the east end with a south aisle and semi-octagonal apse. They also built a south cloister, vestries, chapter house and library. In 1924 a rood screen designed by Sir Ninian J. Comper was installed. The final major additions were made in 1939 by H. O. Tarbolton and Sir Matthew M. Ochterlony, and consisted of a new cloister and two halls. The richly-decorated and furnished interior has a similarly complex history. The church is a large and impressive one, but externally suffers from the absence of a tower or steeple to tie the composition together. The fleche over the crossing, built as part of the campaign of 1849–50, is not visually strong enough for that purpose. The site, at the end of Dunkeld Road, is a strategic one, but the apparatus of modern traffic management has robbed the building of much of its dignity. It merits inclusion here because so many distinguished Anglican and Episcopal architects have contributed to its creation.

122. *Scottish Episcopal Cathedral of the Isles, Millport*

The early steepled Gothic Revival churches showed little acquaintance with genuine medieval prototypes. This church, the centrepiece of the collegiate church of the Holy Spirit, was like St Ninian's, designed by William Butterfield, The complex was built in 1851 for George Boyle, later sixth Earl of Glasgow, as a theological college for the Scottish Episcopal Church, and the design of the church was strongly influenced by the Tractarian movement. The building was given cathedral status in 1876, but two years later the Earl was badly affected by the collapse of the City of Glasgow Bank, and was forced to sell the island of Great Cumbrae to the third Marquess of Bute, a Roman Catholic, who took no interest in the Earl's ambitions. The college buildings now serve as a retreat and conference centre.

123. *Renfield St Stephen's Church of Scotland, Glasgow*

Like the Cathedral of the Isles, this church was designed by an English architect, in this case J. T. Emmett, in the most up-to-date Gothic style. It was constructed for an Independent congregation, dependent for its success on attracting members by fashionable architecture, good preaching and a lively service. It was built in 1849–52 in competition with other churches on the Blythswood estate, developed from the 1830s as an upper-middle-class residential area. It is built in Geometric Gothic style, and has an aisled nave, and a tall, slender spire at its south-west corner. The top part of the steeple collapsed on top of the church in 1998 during a storm, and the building was repaired and re-ordered by CRGP Architects, Glasgow, reopening in 2000. The main worship space is now fully flexible, and more accommodation is provided in the underbuilding. To the west of the church is a church centre, built in the 1960s with money from the sale of the former Renfield Street Church, sold for the building of a department store.

124. St Vincent Street and Milton Free Church, Glasgow

Like Renfield St Stephen's, this building was constructed on the Blythswood estate, but whereas the former was built on a more-or-less level site, St Vincent Street is on a steeply-sloping location. The church was built in 1859 by Alexander 'Greek' Thomson. He was a well-known architect by the mid-1850s, and designed the church for a United Presbyterian congregation who, like the congregation of Renfield St Stephen's, were in competition for members. The high ground of the Gothic Revival having been claimed by other congregations, 'Greek' Thomson adopted a classical form, but with his usual flair amalgamated the temple form with a unique tower, with no classical precedent. To suit the sloping site, he used a massive underbuilding to provide a plinth on which to set his temple. The whole composition has qualities of the picturesque at odds with the formality of the classical, but the building works brilliantly. The interior is even more unusual than the exterior, and much more formal: a broad, rectangular worship space with galleries on three sides, brightly-coloured decoration, and column capitals based on Egyptian models. This is the only one of Thomson's churches to survive intact, and it is a very remarkable building, probably the only church in use in Scotland that is of genuinely international importance.

125. Renfrew Old Parish Church

Though Renfrew was an ancient burgh, it did not grow nearly as fast as Paisley or Glasgow in the eighteenth and nineteenth centuries. It remained a quiet village, with thatched houses and a distinctly vernacular town house, until the 1860s, when industrial growth, especially of shipbuilding, transformed the place into a thriving town. This church, built in 1861–2, is on an old site, as evinced by the survival in the present building of the Motherwell Monument, an altar tomb apparently of late medieval date, and the Ross Vault, a mural tomb of 1633 containing recumbent effigies. The present building was built in 1861–2 to designs by J. T. Rochead of Glasgow, one of the most vigorous and original of mid-nineteenth-century Scottish architects, as a Gothic revival building. It is cruciform, with a tall broach spire at its north-west corner. At the rear is a polygonal session house with a pyramidal roof, designed to resemble a chapter house. The chancel was extended in 1902, by Peter MacGregor Chalmers, without significantly altering the balance of the composition. The church is set in a large, wooded graveyard, with some fine cast-iron railings and gates on its north side, and there are two grave enclosures on the west side of the yard. The principal heritor in the 1860s was Lord Blythswood, whose house, Blythswood House, was to the west of the burgh, and it was probably he who commissioned Rochead. The building is a masterpiece, elegantly simple in a manner rare in Gothic Revival churches. The church should be seen in the round; only in that way can Rochead's mastery of form and massing be appreciated. The detail is there, but it is subdued to the sculptural form of the building. Unfortunately, tree growth is making it difficult to see this church properly, and it would be good to see that addressed.

126. Barclay Church of Scotland, Edinburgh

*I*f Thomson showed one way out of the aesthetic straitjacket of orthodox Gothic Revival, the stretching and deliberate elaboration of conventional Gothic by F. W. Pilkington was another. The Barclay Free church, completed in 1864 with money given by the Misses Barclay, is the most elaborate and distinctive, demonstrating a flair for plastic design unparalleled in Scotland. The exterior is remarkable for the complexity of the roof structure, and for the treatment of the arched openings, most of which have the ogee heads that are distinctive features of Pilkington's designs. The carving of some of the details was never completed, the stones being left 'in block', giving an oddly eerie effect. The interior of the heart-shaped worship space is very lofty, with two tiers of galleries. Curved pews (part of a reordering by Pilkington in 1880) focus on a central pulpit, part of the original Pilkington concept, an auditorium for a great preacher at a time when the most charismatic clergymen had a drawing power as great as a modern television star, and a much more powerful influence. The ceiling has stencilled decoration by James Clark, and the organ case is by Sydney Mitchell. The exceptionally tall spire is a notable landmark.

127. *Catholic Church of The Immaculate Conception, Dundee*

*T*his is another church in which the 'traditional' Gothic Revival is given an entirely new slant, with the chancel given much greater emphasis than usual. It is taller than the nave (which is basilican, with side aisles) and is octagonal in plan, with large windows flooding the interior with light. The altarpiece is flamboyant in style, and was designed by A. B. Wall, Cheltenham. The building itself was designed by Joseph A. Hansom of London and completed in 1866. A feature of the church is a well, 12 metres deep, which is floodlit. The stained glass is by Mayer of Munich. The building was constructed to serve Irish immigrants, many of them women and girls attracted to Lochee, a northern suburb of Dundee, to work in the giant Camperdown Jute Works of Cox Brothers, the largest establishment of its kind in the world.

128. *Innerleithen Parish Church*

*T*his is another example of the work of F. W. Pilkington, built in 1864–7, but on a much smaller scale than the Barclay Church. He won a competition to design the church against David McGibbon and David Bryce. The original intention was to build a tall spire, but this was abandoned, and the stump was left uncapped until 1920, when the present octagonal louvred cupola was installed. A chancel was added in 1888–9, to designs by J. McIntyre Henry, to accommodate an organ. The east front features the ogee-headed windows characteristic of Pilkington, and three large foiled windows in the gable head. Below these is the stump of a ninth-century cross found on the site of the parish church which preceded this one. When the Pilkington church was built, Innerleithen was developing as a woollen manufacturing centre, and also as a tourist centre, as the town features as 'St Ronan's Well' in Sir Walter Scott's novel of that name.

129. *St Andrew's Scottish Episcopal Church, Kelso*

Sir R. Rowand Anderson was one of the most prolific of late nineteenth-century church architects in Scotland. This is one of his smallest, but most attractive churches, completed in 1868 and tucked away in a side street close to the centre of the burgh of Kelso, itself a notably pleasing place. From the south bank of the river Tweed, its steeple, simpler than originally intended, forms a distinctive part of the skyline of the town. Anderson has packed into this tiny building an amount of thought and incident which could have been adequate for a much larger church, and yet avoided undue fussiness. His larger churches are sometimes impressive rather than lovable, but this one is both. Internally, there is a stone reredos in the chancel, which has stencilled decoration. The nave has a scissor-beam roof, and circular clerestory windows. The east window has stained glass by Rowand Anderson, and there is also glass by Douglas Strachan.

130. *St Andrew's Scottish Episcopal Cathedral, Inverness*

The second new Scots cathedral built since the Reformation, St Andrew's is an impressive church on a fine riverside site. Because of tree growth, it is not as clearly visible as originally intended. Its most striking features are the twin towers flanking the main entrance, which were originally intended to be capped with tall spires. It was designed by Alexander Ross, a leading Inverness architect of the time, and built between 1866 and 1869. The sculpture on the west front is by Earp of London. The entrance leads into a narthex, with the baptistry on the left, in the base of the south-west tower. The font, in the form of an angel holding a scallop shell, was made by James F. Redfern, and is based on one in a Copenhagen church. There is a glazed stone screen between the narthex and the nave. The nave is aisled, with monolithic, red, Peterhead granite columns, and is separated from the choir by a wooden screen designed by Sir Robert Lorimer, and installed in 1923 as a war memorial. The choir is also aisled. with a panelled wagon roof decorated with stencilling. The choir stalls date from 1909. The altar, on a trefoil plan, was installed when the church was built, as was the reredos, of Caen stone and marble and made by Earp. The pulpit is of a design by Thomas Ross, and also an original feature.

Altogether, the building has a magnificence unexpected in a town which was a stronghold of presbyterianism in many forms. Its scale and elaboration are clear indicators of the metropolitan status that Inverness assumed in the later nineteenth century, largely on account of its significance as a railway centre, and recently reinforced and recognised by the award of city status.

131. Dingwall Free Church

Of the many churches built for the Free Church of Scotland between the Disruption in 1843 and the Union of the Free and United Presbyterian churches in 1900, most passed to the new United Free Church. Most of the exceptions were either fairly small buildings, or in northern Scotland. Two of these stand out. One is Free North in Inverness – the 'Free Church Cathedral', massive in scale, an important landmark beside the river Ness, but very conventionally Gothic in design. The other is this one in Dingwall, county town of Ross and Cromarty, also built – in 1867–70 – on a large scale, but of a much more intriguing design. The architect was John Rhind of Edinburgh. Its most distinctive feature is the elongated cupola, which sits comfortably on its tower, but which was constructed after the foundations proved inadequate to support the intended spire. Internally, it has a horse-shoe gallery. There are stained-glass windows, dating from the construction of the building, by Ballantine and Co.

132. Dysart Parish Church

This little church is one of the first buildings of the Second Romanesque Revival, cruciform in plan, with apsidal ends to the transepts and chancel, and a squat tower with short spire. It was built in 1872–4 as Dysart Free Church. The massing of the building is comparable with that of St Monans (see above), but the detailing is clearly modelled on genuine twelfth-century work, perhaps at Leuchars. Unfortunately, tree growth currently prevents full appreciation of the subtlety of the design. The architects were Campbell Douglas and Sellars, of Glasgow. Recently some stencilled decoration by Charles Rennie Mackintosh has been uncovered. When the church was built, Dysart, now an eastern suburb of Kirkcaldy, was an independent burgh, with nearby coal mines and a busy harbour engaged both in shipping coal and in general trade

133. *Palmerston Place Church of Scotland, Edinburgh*

*T*he epitome of a fashionable West End church, Palmerston Place was built in 1873–5 for a United Presbyterian congregation which moved from Rose Street, in the first New Town, as that area became more commercial than residential. The new building was constructed on a street frontage site on the Wester Coates estate, being developed as a high-class residential area by the Heriot Trust. The design of the church, by Peddie and Kinnear, reflects its street frontage position, with all the external emphasis being placed on its eastern show front. This has been compared (in the *Buildings of Scotland: Edinburgh*) to the front of the church of Saint-Sulpice in Paris, and has a broad flight of steps leading to an Italian arcaded centre with flanking stair towers, capped by copper-roofed cupolas. The entrance doors are set back behind the arcade. Inside there is a large vestibule, behind which is a D-plan worship space, with the gallery supported on red, Peterhead granite columns, carried up to support round-headed arches. The clerestory windows are also arcaded. The flat ceiling is decorated with Greek motifs. The focal point of the seating, which is curved on the ground floor as well as in the gallery, is an ornate Renaissance pulpit, and above it there is a broad 'chancel' arch in which an organ case, in similar style, is set. These fittings were designed by J. M. Dick Peddie and G. Washington Browne, and installed in 1901. Palmerston is one of the greatest preaching churches in Scotland, admirably designed for that purpose. Just as in Rose Street, however, the once-residential Wester Coates estate has become largely commercial and administrative, and the congregation is largely a gathered one.

134. Queen's Park Baptist Church, Glasgow

The first church here was built in 1873, as Camphill United Presbyterian Church, to serve the tenement flats and terrace houses being constructed to the north and west. This survives as the church hall, and was supplanted by a much grander place of worship in 1875–8, designed by William Leiper. This is the finest of Leiper's four major churches, the others being Dowanhill and Hyndland in Glasgow, and St Columba's, Kilmacolm. Though not an innovative design (it was based on that of J. L. Pearson's St Augustine's Church, Kilburn, London, and ultimately on the French Gothic of Normandy), it is a very satisfying one, in particular in the way in which the generously-proportioned spire (completed in 1883) relates to the situation of the church on the edge of Queen's Park. The detailing of the entrance front is also nobly conceived, with low-relief carvings of an angel, by John Mossman, above the doorway, and more angels in the tympanum of the porch arch. As built, it had elaborate stencilling on the walls and ceiling, of which the golden flowers on the ceiling (a typical Leiper feature) can still be seen. Latterly known as Camphill Queen's Park Church, it was abandoned by the Church of Scotland in the mid-1990s, in favour of its much less accomplished neighbour, the former Queen's Park West Church. Camphill Queen's Park was taken over by Queen's Park Baptist Church to replace, as their principal place of worship, their Romanesque church in Queen's Drive, and the interior was adapted to suit in 1998–9.

135. Kelvinside Hillhead Parish Church, Glasgow

If Camphill Queen's Park is a fairly conservative design, the contemporary Hillhead Parish Church is not. Its precursor was a corrugated-iron church built as a chapel of ease of Govan Parish Church. Modelled on the Sainte Chapelle Church in Paris, the present building was the subject of a design competition in which Leiper took part. The winner was James Sellars, one of the finest late nineteenth-century Glasgow architects, but the church as built in 1875–6 is said to incorporate features from Leiper's entry. The low-relief angels on the west front, and the octagonal buttress towers with their short spires are features found in Leiper's churches. The building is on an elongated D-plan, and there are no full-height columns in the interior, which is lit by tall windows with geometric

tracery. The ceiling is timber-lined, to resemble a groined vault. The stained glass is exceptionally fine, with windows by Sir Edward Burne-Jones and Morris and Co. (1893), Cottier and Co. (1893–1903), William Meikle and Sons (1917) and Sadie McLellan (1958). The rest of the windows are leaded, with pale green, gold and pink panes in an abstract design anticipating the Art Deco style of the inter-war years. Some, at least, of the plaster frieze below the windows was covered in Aesthetic Movement stencilling, with panels lined out to resemble ashlar masonry. The chancel area was remodelled as a war memorial by Peter MacGregor Chalmers in about 1921, with memorial tablets set in blind arcading on either side of the simple marble Communion table, behind which is a dossle, a reredos with velvet brocade hangings in blue and gold, designed to give vertical emphasis. Sets of four elders' seats flank the war memorial arcades. The low pulpit, on the left of the chancel, is a richly-carved Gothic structure. At the rear of the church there is a gallery which now accommodates the organ console and the choir, and below that is an inner entrance porch and a baptistery, with an elaborate timber font and font cover, an unusual feature in a presbyterian church. These features were installed in 1926 to mark the jubilee of the building of the church. The small stained-glass windows in the baptistery date from 1928. The organ, by H. Willis and Son ('Father' Willis), is contemporary with the building, but was enlarged in 1930, when the present richly-carved organ case was installed. Because the church is on a sloping site, the halls are in the underbuilding. What is not obvious is that owing to mining below the building, the foundations of the church are taken down to solid rock, some 13 metres below ground level. Hillhead Parish was originally part of the very large Govan parish. The congregation united with the nearby Kelvinside Church (a former Free church) in the 1970s, which still stands at the corner of Great Western Road and Byres Road, and has recently been converted into an entertainment complex. The church sits well in the residential terraces it was designed to serve. The articulation of the exterior is thoroughly convincing, and the interior is striking. The stained-glass windows are all of the highest quality, and give a feeling of richness to the worship space. They do, however, distract the attention of the viewer from the elegant simplicity of the architecture, as does the Macgregor Chalmers remodelling of the chancel area. But these are quibbles, for by any standards this is an outstanding building.

136. *St John's Church of Scotland, Dunoon*

*T*his large building was built in 1876–7 to replace the original Dunoon Free Church of 1843, and was designed to accommodate the large number of well-to-do Glasgow families who came down to Dunoon for the summer. The architect was R. A. Bryden of Glasgow. It is, like Camphill Queen's Park Church (see above), in Normandy-Gothic style. Though less accomplished than that church, it is a fascinating and impressive structure, on a steeply-sloping site, which increases its apparent size. Internally, it has a horse-shoe gallery behind arcades with cast-iron columns, on an awe-inspiring scale. The galleries have gableted roofs, with plaster-vaulted ceilings. The central pulpit is flanked by raised, raked choir galleries, as far as I know a unique feature, put in when the organ was installed in 1895. There are stained-glass windows by Stephen Adam and Gordon Webster. A rear entrance porch gives access at gallery level.

137. *St Mary's Scottish Episcopal Cathedral, Edinburgh*

*T*his building is included here essentially because of its colossal scale and remarkable history. It was built in stages from legacies left by two maiden ladies, the Misses Walker, who had profited handsomely from the development of the Easter Coates estate, round the site of the cathedral. A design competition was held, in which the winner was Sir George Gilbert Scott, an architect noted for the quantity of building he could deliver for a given price. The exceptionally-large structure, on a cruciform plan, was constructed in three stages. The body with a central tower and spire, and a pair of western towers, was built between 1874 and 1879. The octagonal chapter house at the north-east corner was added in 1890–1, and finally the spires were added to the western towers in 1913–17, completing the original design. The western towers were apparently inspired by the competition entry by Alexander Ross of Inverness (see St Andrew's Cathedral, Inverness, above). Adjacent to the north transept is Easter Coates House, the small tower house of 1615 which was the home of the Misses Walker. It became the choir school for the cathedral in 1887, and in 1903 the north wing was remodelled by George Henderson. In the extensive grounds of the cathedral is the Song School, a hall designed by J. Oldrid Scott, with crow-stepped gables and a fleche. Inside there is a plaster tunnel-vaulted ceiling. The walls have mural paintings by Phoebe Traquair, the noted Edinburgh mural artist, on the theme of the Benedicite. To the north of the Song School is the Walpole Hall, designed by Sir Robert Lorimer and J. F. Matthew and completed in 1933, with Cape-Dutch gables and dormers.

138. Priestfield Church of Scotland, Edinburgh

Completed in 1879 as Rosehall United Presbyterian Church, and built to serve a growing middle-class area, the design of this building was, as was popular at the time, the subject of a competition. The winners were Sutherland and Walker, with an elaborate Lombardic Romanesque composition. This is a striking style briefly popular in the Edinburgh area with denominations that did not like Gothic because of its medieval associations, or because it was becoming a hackneyed style. It is characterised by extensive use of round-headed arches in a variety of combinations. In this case the west front has flanking towers, and a central rose window, a common feature in United Presbyterian churches. Internally, there is a U-plan gallery, with Lombardic carving on the gallery fronts. The walls are divided into arcaded bays by pilasters with waterleaf capitals painted gold. The pitch-pine pulpit is also decorated with Lombardic carving. The design of this building is very foreign to modern eyes, but at the time of its construction John Ruskin had made all things Italian popular, and well-to-do people – and students of architecture – often visited Italy. In the circumstances it is not surprising that this striking and distinctive style had a brief vogue.

139. Barony Church, Dalswinton

An example of the corrugated-iron churches which were popular in the late nineteenth and early twentieth centuries with congregations of limited means, or as a preliminary to building a more permanent structure. As they could be dismantled and re-erected, some were used on several sites. This one was built in 1881 by the owners of the Dalswinton estate as a chapel of ease for estate workers, and was brought up by rail from London in sections. It is particularly complete, with its original pitch-pine fittings.

140. *Galashiels Old Parish Church and St Paul's*

Galashiels developed as the largest centre of tweed manufacture in Scotland in the second half of the nineteenth century, and the scale of this church is an indication of the prosperity of the town in that period. It was built as St Paul's Church in 1879–81 to complement the old parish church of 1813, by that time far too small for the growing population of the burgh. The minister of the parish church and his assistant took alternate services in the two buildings (this arrangement is still in operation in Elgin, with St Giles' and St Columba's churches). Designed by George Henderson, it is a large Geometric Gothic building on a T-plan, with a tall spire, completed in 1885, at the north-west corner. The nave is aisled, with red, Peterhead granite columns in the arcades, and there are transept galleries under gabled roofs. The main roof is an open timber one. An organ was installed from the start. There are some good stained-glass windows, including a memorial to Queen Victoria, installed in 1902, and some by Douglas Strachan. A porch was added in 1902, and some of the ornamental details of the spire have since been removed. This is an assured composition on an excellent open site, with a background of the wooded hills which border the valley in which Galashiels is situated.

141. *Wellington Church of Scotland, Glasgow*

The Wellington congregation started in 1792 as an Anti-burgher secession church, an offshoot of a congregation in Duke Street which had become too large for its building. The first church was in Cheapside Street, Anderston, at that time a growing hand-loom weaving community at a little distance from Glasgow. After the formation of the United Secession Church in 1820, they built a new classical church in Wellington Street in 1827. In the 1880s the congregation, by then part of the United Presbyterian Church, decided to move to a site in the burgh of Hillhead, University Avenue, opposite the new University of Glasgow, and on the edge of a middle-class suburb of the city. To make a link with their old church they built the new one, completed in 1884, in classical style, too, but much more elaborately, modelling it on the Roman temple of the Maison Carrée at Nîmes. The new church was designed by T. L. Watson, and was one of the last classical churches built in Scotland. Being set into a slope, the approach is by flights of steps to a plinth on which the Corinthian portico sits. Internally, the building has a broad, rectangular worship space, with galleries on three sides, and a central pulpit and organ. The ceiling is coffered. The chancel area was remodelled in the 1920s as a war memorial, to designs by Sir D. Y. Cameron, the well-known landscape painter. The Communion table and chairs from this scheme remain in place. but the choir seats which flanked the chancel have recently been moved to the back of the building, at the sides. The fittings are of very high quality, as the congregation was a wealthy one. As the church has substantial underbuilding it has been possible to excavate out a space which is now used as a cafe for university students.

142. St Andrew's Parish Church, Moffat

Moffat had been recognised as a spa town since the late eighteenth century, and was also an important staging post on the main road from Carlisle and north-west England to Edinburgh. After the opening of the Caledonian Railway from Carlisle to Glasgow and Edinburgh in 1848, the road traffic declined, but the Caledonian opened a branch railway from Beattock in 1869. This boosted the attraction of the place as a holiday resort for the upper middle classes, who flocked to the hotels which had been designed for the coach traffic. Large villas were also built for wealthy residents who had retired, or who could afford to travel by rail to business in Glasgow or Edinburgh. St Andrew's Parish Church (1884) and a rival Free (later United Free) church were built on a scale and with a magnificence appropriate to the numbers and affluence of the residents of and visitors to the town. St Andrew's was designed by John Starforth, who specialised in large, ornate, late Gothic revival churches. There are other examples of his work in Dumfries, Kelso and Nairn. Features of his work are the use of rock-faced masonry, and the curving of the gallery staircases which flank the central tower and entrance. These treatments are both clearly evident here. What is unusual is the incorporation of a turret into the tower, making it asymmetrical. The church is set in open grounds on the south-western approach to the town, almost opposite the site of the railway station, and with its monumental quality sets the tone of the Victorian heyday of this resort town.

143. St Leonard's-in-the-Fields and Trinity Parish Church, Perth

*T*his is probably the first large church in the country with a design that drew inspiration from the late Scots Gothic of the late fifteenth and sixteenth centuries. It was designed by J. J. Stevenson, a Glasgow architect who spent most of his career in London, and it was completed in 1885 for a wealthy Free Church congregation. The features that are most explicitly Scots are the massive buttresses, the curvilinear tracery and the crown steeple, modelled on that at St Giles, Edinburgh. These features give the building a robust, almost assertive effect, disguising the very conventional internal layout. It was built on the edge of the North Inch, one of the two large, public, open spaces which add so much to the character and amenity of Perth, and which gives the church an excellent setting.

144. St Sophia's Catholic Church, Galston

*T*he family of the marquesses of Bute, with their close connections with the Scots royal family, became members of the Church of Scotland at the Reformation, but in the late nineteenth century the Third Marquess converted to Roman Catholicism. The family estates included land in South Wales and at Cumnock, Ayrshire, and they made a great deal of money from the mining and shipping of coal. The Marquess used some of his vast fortune to build Roman Catholic churches in the west of Scotland, and this one, built in 1885–6, is one of the most unusual. Domes are rare in Scottish churches, and brick was an odd material to use for the exterior of a church in the 1880s. Its designer, Sir R. Rowand Anderson (possibly in this case working with Robert Weir Schultz), was, however, fond of building the internal faces of walls in brick. It is said that the building was modelled on the great Byzantine church of St Sophia in Istanbul, but it is really only the name and the concept of a domed building that they share. At the time this church was built, Galston was one of the three Irvine Valley towns – along with Darvel, and Newmilns – that had recently replaced their hand-loom weaving industries with the making of lace curtains and tablecloths by machine, and were accordingly prospering.

145. *St Molio's Church of Scotland, Shiskine*

*T*he idea of constructing modest but well-detailed churches, in contrast to large Gothic or classical buildings, had its origins in churches like St Serf's, Dysart, but only began to be taken seriously in the late 1880s. St Molio's, opened in 1889, is the first of a series of low churches with squat towers designed by J. J. Burnet (see Gardner Memorial Church, Brechin, below). These incorporated some English Arts and Crafts features, in this case the porch, the oversailing eaves and the use of reddish Rosemary tiles as a roof-covering. The building is constructed in a warm, red sandstone. At the north end of the church, a late-medieval graveslab depicting a priest has been inserted into a buttress, to represent St Molio. At the time the church was built, Arran was developing into a high-class holiday island, and St Molio's was the church for Blackwaterfoot, a popular place for golfing holidays.

146. *Southwick Church of Scotland*

*T*his is another modest church, this time fairly closely comparable to St Serf's, Dysart. Like that, it is scholarly Romanesque in style, though in this case only the chancel has an apsidal end. It was designed by Kinnear and Peddie, essentially for Sir Mark Stewart of Southwick House, and built in 1889–91. The short tower, with its solid parapet, may derive from St Monans (see above). Other churches in this style are at Dalton, Dumfriesshire and Abington, South Lanarkshire. The interior is laid out for Scoto-catholic worship, with the Communion table in the chancel, which has contemporary stained glass in its little, round-headed windows, and which is approached through an arch with chevron detail, flanked on the left by a Jacobean pulpit, and on the right by a neo-Norman font. The nave has a timber wagon roof, and 'Arts and Crafts' oil-lamp fittings. The Southwick church is essentially a 'chapel of ease' and, like St Molio's, probably catered for summer visitors, in this case to the village of Caulkerbush.

15. Oakshaw Trinity Church, Paisley (59). Built as the High Kirk, and seen looking up Stoney Brae, this large church was opened in 1756 to cope with the expanding population of the textile burgh. The spire, with its clock, was added in 1770 by the Town Council, and is a notable landmark.

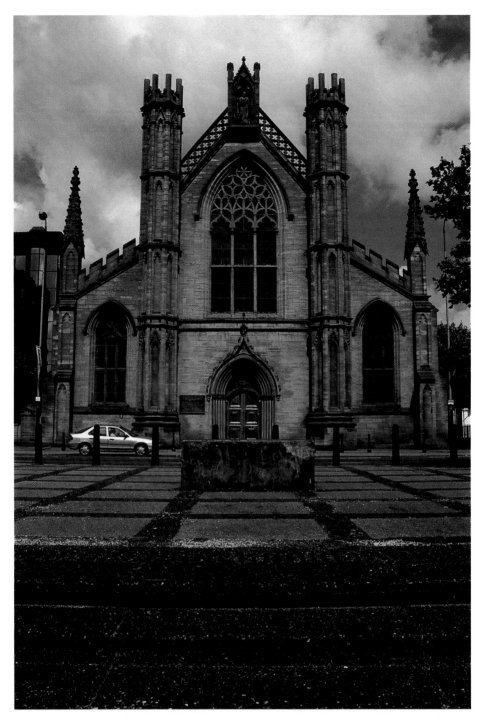

16. St Andrew's Catholic Cathedral, Glasgow (91). The first Catholic church built in the west of Scotland since the Reformation, this was designed as a dominant feature of the river frontage, by James Gillespie Graham. It was completed in 1816, and adapted as the Cathedral of the Archdiocese of Glasgow in 1889.

17. St John's Scottish Episcopal Church, Edinburgh (95). Designed by William Burn, and opened in 1817, this striking church is notable for its plaster fan vaulting, modelled on English Perpendicular examples, and for its stained glass. The form of the chancel seen here dates from 1879–82.

18. Dunfermline Abbey Church (97). On the site of the choir of the mediaeval abbey church, this large Perpendicular Gothic church was built in 1821 to serve the growing population of the burgh. It covers the grave of King Robert the Bruce, whose name is set in the parapet of the tower.

19. Catholic Church of the Immaculate Conception, Dundee (127). Completed in 1866, to serve Irish immigrants working in local jute mills, this unique church was designed by Joseph Hansom of London. This view shows how the interior is finished in two colours of sandstone and a yellow facing brick.
Crown Copyright: Royal Commission on the Ancient and Historical Monuments of Scotland

20. Palmerston Place Church, Edinburgh (133). This church was opened in 1875 in the fashionable West End. This view shows the shallow apse, organ case and pulpit designed by J. M. Dick Peeddie and G. Washington Browne and installed in 1901, when organs were becoming fashionable.

21. Cranshaws Parish Church (151). Designed by a local architect, George Fortune of Duns, this delightful little church was opened in 1899. It was built at the expense of Andrew Smith of Cranshaws, whose pew, entered from outside. is on the left in this view. The semi-circular chancel and chancel arch are typical of the then-fashionable Romanesque revival.

22. St Mary's Scottish Episcopal Cathedral, Edinburgh (137). The largest Gothic Revival church in Scotland, St Mary's was designed by Sir George Gilbert Scott, and paid for by two sisters, the Misses Walker. The western steeples, seen here, were finished in 1917, 43 years after building started.

23. Lowson Memorial Church, Forfar (163).
An exceptional example of Scots Gothic
Revival, this church, designed by A Marshall
Mackenzie of Aberdeen, opened in 1914.
This view shows how light floods into the
nave from the clerestory, and the organ,
perched on a free-standing gallery.

**24. St Columba's Catholic Church, Glasgow
(173).** Completed in 1941 to designs by
Gillespie, Kidd and Coia, St Columba's has a
reinforced concrete frame. This view along
the south aisle show the pure elegance which
this form of construction could produce.

25. St Andrew's Catholic Church, Livingston (183). One of the most original post-war churches is this
New Town building, designed by Alison, Hutchison and Partners, and opened in 1970. The exterior walls
form a series of overlapping curves, with glazing in the spaces between them.

147. St Cuthbert's Parish Church, Edinburgh

*T*he medieval parish of St Cuthbert's was probably established in the twelfth century, possibly by David I when he reorganised church administration in Scotland. It was a two-chamber church, with a long nave and a shorter choir. There was a tower on the south side of the nave, as at Dunblane Cathedral (see above). After the Reformation the church was split into two sections, the nave becoming the 'Little Kirk', with little alteration to the fabric, and the choir being enlarged at various times. In 1772 the building was declared unsafe, and a competition was held to design a replacement. The winner was James Weir of Tollcross, and the new church was built in 1773–5. It was on a rectangular plan, with two tiers of galleries, and a pedimented projecting bay on the west end, containing the gallery stairs. A classical clock tower with a Georgian steeple was added in 1789–90, to designs by Alexander Stevens, at the same time as the burial ground was extended to the north. The body of the 'new' church became unsafe in the 1880s, and Hippolyte J. Blanc was commissioned to deal with the problem. His initial intention was to recase the building, as had been done with St Giles, Edinburgh (see above). But instead, the building was rebuilt in 1892–5 on a much larger scale, retaining the tower and steeple of 1789–90. The aesthetic relationship between steeple and the rebuilt body of the church is distinctly uneasy, and it is probably just as well that tree growth has hidden much of the church from distant view. The east end (which can be seen from West Princes Street Gardens) is the best elevation, with baroque towers flanking the enormous domed apse, giving a rather Byzantine feel to the building. The unease does not continue into the interior, which is extraordinarily effective, even though the back of the worship space has been partitioned off to form a large vestibule. The worship space itself is cruciform, with a U-plan gallery in the nave, supported on modified Corinthian columns. The broad chancel, with a semicircular vault, ends in a semicircular apse, with its domed ceiling, which is lit at clerestory level. The roofs of the chancel and apse and the spandrels of the chancel arch are all decorated in mosaic, and there is a large painting by John Duncan (of St Cuthbert on Lindisfarne) on the west wall, above the gallery. The most striking feature of the apse is, however, a band of high-relief alabaster sculpture based on Leonardo da Vinci's *Last Supper*. This was designed by Blanc, and made in Lichfield by Bridgeman, in 1906–8. The building is laid out for Scoto-catholic worship, with a white marble Communion table in the apse, enriched with green marble, porphyry and semi-precious stones. The pulpit incorporates red marble columns from a church in Verona. These were designed by Blanc, as were the pews, choir stalls and the elders' seats in the apse. The extraordinary font was designed by Thomas Armstrong, Keeper of Fine Art in what is now the Victoria and Albert Museum, and made in 1907–8. The water in the font is contained in a trough round the edge, the centre being occupied by a marble copy of Michelangelo's *Bruges Madonna*. The enormous organ was installed in 1899, by R. Hope-Jones, with pipes in the north transept, and on both sides of the chancel. The effect of all this richness of detail can aptly be described as splendid. Individually furnishings and details may be over-rich but, for me at least, the synthesis is remarkably effective, a very acceptable reaction to the emphasis on the Gothic so characteristic of late nineteenth-century Scottish church design.

148. *Thomas Coats Memorial Baptist Church, Paisley*

*T*his church, like St Mary's Episcopal Cathedral and St Cuthbert's, is at the opposite end of the scale of late nineteenth-century churches to St Molio's and Southwick. What the Clarks were to the east end of Paisley and to the restoration of the Abbey (see above), the Coats family were to the west end of the town, and to this church. Thomas Coats, the stay-at-home brother responsible for production at the Ferguslie Thread Mills and for the design of the equipment used in the company's overseas factories, was a leading member of one of the Baptist churches in Paisley. Following his death the surviving members of the family resolved to build in his memory the Baptist church to end all Baptist churches. The Thomas Coats Memorial Baptist Church is evidence that they succeeded. The architect, Hippolyte Blanc of Edinburgh, chose to design a cathedral-like structure at the west end of the High Street, on a sloping site. The church, completed in 1894, is approached by a gigantic flight of stairs, the largest in Scotland. The red sandstone building is cruciform, with a crown steeple, and is richly decorated both inside and out, with some notable stained glass, marble and alabaster. The chancel and crossing are vaulted in stone, with painted panels. There are high-relief sculptured alabaster panels below the windows at the end of the chancel, and the marble pulpit also has carved alabaster panels. The marble font, for adult baptism by total immersion, is behind the pulpit. The nave is aisled, with flying buttresses, a feature more French than Scots. The timber roofs of the nave and transepts have stencilled decoration. The richness and quality of the decoration is carried through into tiny details, such as door handles. There is ancillary accommodation, recently modernised, in the underbuilding of the church. It is ironic that a man who appears to have loved the simplicity of mid-nineteenth-century Baptist thought should be commemorated in this extraordinarily elaborate way. The Coats family also contributed substantially to the building of two other large churches in Paisley: St James' and Wallneuk (see below). There are fine statues of Thomas Coats and Sir Peter Coats at Paisley Cross.

149. *St Patrick's Catholic Church, Coatbridge*

*T*he Roman Catholic population of the west of Scotland expanded markedly in the late nineteenth century, and became more prosperous. This created the need for more and larger churches. The archdiocese of Glasgow, at the time responsible for the whole of west central Scotland, chose the firm of Pugin and Pugin, successors to Augustus Welby Pugin, pioneer of the Gothic Revival, to design a large number of churches which bore a close family resemblance to each other. These are all basilican, with aisled naves and semi-octagonal apsidal chancels. They were dressed up to look different from each other, with different treatment of windows. One (Holy Cross, Glasgow) is even in Byzantine Romanesque. Some are built of cream sandstone, others of red. St Patrick's, built of cream sandstone and opened in 1896, is in the heart of Coatbridge, by the 1890s largely a Roman Catholic town. The site was given by William Baird and Co., proprietors of the Gartsherrie Iron Works, the town's largest employer. It is a typical example of the work of Pugin and Pugin, but with more restrained detail than some, for instance St Augustine's, at the west end of the burgh. The elaborate Gothic reredos of what was until Vatican II the altar has been retained, and there are similar but smaller versions in the side chapels at the end of the aisles. The chancel has painted decoration on its ceiling. An enclosed centenary chapel has been created at the south end of the east aisle. The effect is primarily that of a pre-Vatican II 'traditional' Roman Catholic church, immensely impressive and dignified. The main street at this point has been pedestrianised, and both tree planting and hard landscaping undertaken, in a way which enhances the monumental effect of the gabled front of the building.

150. *Crichton Memorial Church, Dumfries*

*I*n 1823 a Dumfries man, Dr James Crichton, who was physician to the East India Company, died and left a large sum to his widow with the instruction that it was to be used for charitable purposes. His widow initially wanted to found a university, but found this impractical, and instead established a pioneering mental hospital, which became a model institution, providing accommodation for well-to-do patients as well as for the less well-off. The hospital was greatly enlarged in the 1890s to cope with the reorganisation of mental health care at that time. The new buildings were designed by Sydney Mitchell, an Edinburgh architect who established a reputation for hospital design. He was also commissioned to design a church for the hospital, which was completed between 1890 and 1897. There are similarities to the Coats Memorial church, especially in the use of the sloping site and in the adoption of a cruciform plan, with a central tower. The building is, however, much less elaborately detailed. It is in an open setting, which allows the church to be seen in the round. The style is Geometric Gothic, and the building has a long nave and a massive pinnacled tower, of cathedral-like proportions, over the crossing. The effect is of a settled inevitability, quite different to the soaring ambition of the Coats Memorial. The exterior stone is from Locharbriggs, with its distinctive, rich, red colour, the colour of Dumfries. The interior, finished in the paler and pinker Gatelawbridge stone, is impressive in its simplicity, which is enhanced by the remarkable leaded-glass windows by Oscar Paterson, a Glasgow stained-glass artist. These have very little colour, allowing light to flood into the church. Changes in the treatment of mental illness have resulted in much of the hospital becoming redundant, and in a very enlightened move Dumfries and Galloway region, before local government reorganisation in 1996, established the Crichton Trust, charged with finding productive uses for the obsolete buildings. Dumfries now has its university, a college of both Glasgow and Paisley universities, and the non-denominational church, no longer needed to serve the hospital, is now a popular place for wedding services.

151. *Cranshaws Parish Church*

Situated in a remote upland part of Berwickshire, this may be an ancient worship site. The building contains a low-relief sculpture of the Scots royal arms, which according to tradition were given by James VI to the parish minister, the Rev. Alexander Swinton, after he had neglected his duty (in the presence of the king) to pray for the royal family. The present church was designed by George Fortune, of Duns, and was completed in 1899. It replaced an earlier one built in 1789, part of the walls of which are embedded in the base of this one. The current church is an exceptional example of the second Romanesque Revival, with scholarly detailing. Internally, the church has a nave and apse-ended chancel. To the left of the east end of the nave is a tiny laird's loft, approached through an external door. The timber roof of the nave has stencilled decoration on the principal rafters. The interior has an intimate and sheltering feel to it, appropriate in a building set in an exposed and often bleak landscape. The rebuilding was paid for by the then laird, Andrew Smith of Cranshaws.

152. *Gardner Memorial Church of Scotland, Brechin*

This is both another memorial church (to Alexander Gardner, Minister) and another of J. J. Burnet's 'low line' churches (see St Molio's, Shiskine, above). It was built in 1896–1900 on the outskirts of the town centre of Brechin, opposite the railway station and a small wooded park. The site slopes slightly, and the church is at the lower end, on the left facing the complex. The dominant feature is the large tower, big enough to house the stair to the small gallery at the rear of the nave, with the body of the church extending to the rear. To the right of the tower is the main entrance to the complex, with the halls ranged along the street in a low range. The church and halls enclose a courtyard, containing a garden with raised beds, and there is an open corridor on this side of the hall block. The church is split into two longitudinal bays, with an arcade dividing them. The nave and chancel are to the left, the chancel being arranged for Scoto-catholic worship, with Communion table at the end, pulpit to the left, and choir stalls facing each other on either side of the chancel. The organ is at the 'east' end of the right-hand bay. It is not a large church, and this arrangement gives a feeling of intimacy. The open-timber roof is of complex construction, incorporating scissors trusses. Above the entrance to the chancel there is a vestigial rood screen. The woodwork is all in straight-grained pine, stained a dark greenish colour, and detailed with remarkable refinement. The external detailing, too, of this pinkish sandstone building is exquisite, and also humorous, with grotesque masks at eaves level. Altogether, this is a very pleasing and thoughtful building, on a human scale, and arguably the best of Burnet's churches.

153. *Greyfriars John Knox Church of Scotland, Aberdeen*

*M*arischal College was founded in 1593 and originally located in the former Greyfriars monastery in the city centre of Aberdeen. It was extended in the seventeenth century, and again in 1837. The eastern side of the college was formed by the late Scots Gothic church of the Greyfriars, built in 1518–32 under the supervision of Alexander Galloway, minister of Kinkell, near Inverurie. In the early 1890s, with the start of government funding for universities, Aberdeen University (formed in 1860 by amalgamating the earlier King's College with Marischal) needed to expand, and eventually decided to rebuild Marischal on a massive scale and in a very elaborate manner, to designs by A. Marshall Mackenzie, the leading Aberdeen architect of the day. At the time the city's granite industry was flourishing, and the new college buildings were built of this stone, which is very resistant to weathering. As an advertisement for the virtuosity of the city's craftsmen, the opportunity was taken to give the buildings a complex skyline, with a forest of pinnacles. The original intention was to restore the Greyfriars Church as the University church. Eventually it was decided to rebuild it at the same time as the college proper, and in a complementary manner, balancing the entrance block further north along Broad Street. The new church was completed in 1903. The tower has a forest of pinnacles surrounding a slender crocketted steeple, which sounds over-elaborate, but has in fact a magical effect with a lightness absent from most Gothic Revival architecture. The east window incorporates tracery from the sixteenth-century building, and the wood-panelled chancel has choir pews with the ends from predecessors of 1690. The church is arranged for Scoto-catholic worship, and is notably light and airy, with stained glass by C. E. Kempe. The Willis organ is the original instrument of 1903. Aberdeen University has now moved out of Marischal College, and the buildings are being converted to other uses. The complex remains central Aberdeen's most distinctive piece of townscape. The present name derives from a recent union with the former John Knox Church.

154. *St Mary's Scottish Episcopal Church, Kirriemuir*

*T*his church was completed in 1903 and replaced one of 1797, destroyed by fire. The eighteenth-century building was classical, but its replacement is a red sandstone structure in the 'Arts and Crafts' style. It is the only complete church in Scotland designed by Sir Ninian Comper, the son of an Episcopal clergyman in Aberdeen. The building is dominated by a bulky tower at its west end, with a stair tower at its north-west corner. The furnishings were designed by Comper, and there is good stained glass by Comper and by William Wilson in windows with innovative tracery, a free interpretation of the Flamboyant style of the early sixteenth century. One of the Comper windows is a memorial to his father.

155. *Eastbank Church of Scotland, Glasgow*

*T*his church, in the centre of Shettleston (at the time an industrial suburb of Glasgow), was originally commissioned by a United Presbyterian congregation. However, by the time it was completed the United Presbyterian and Free churches had united to become the United Free Church. A new and elaborate Church of Scotland church, now Shettleston Old, had been built nearby a few years earlier, and Eastbank was probably designed partly to compete with that building. The first part of the complex was the hall, opened in 1899 and used as a place of worship while the church was being built. Both were designed by W. F. McGibbon. The exterior is neat enough, with the entrance front facing south, flanked on the west by the hall, and on the east by a tower with an octagonal steeple set behind its parapet. The steeple and the roof of the church are both covered with Rosemary tiles, which, with the red sandstone (Locharbriggs and Corncockle, both from Dumfriesshire) of the masonry, give the building a bright, cheerful appearance. The broad window above the entrance, the late Gothic leaf carving round the doorway, and the Glasgow-style malleable-iron railings are the only hints that this is an unusually-interesting church. The interior is, in a very real sense, a shock. Instead of the neat, bright, but bland United Free interiors characteristic of the early 1900s, the worship space is dark, rich and compact, with layer upon layer of thought-provoking ideas. It is an immensely-powerful space, a space with that sense of the 'other' that when present in a church compels contemplation of the nature of the divine. The details, fine in themselves, are subservient to the totality. Painted decoration on the panelled ceiling, inscribed with the *Te Deum*, gallery fronts in stained timber with exquisitely-detailed tracery panels, an organ-case forming a canopy over the panelled pulpit and Communion table, and the massive Arts and Crafts table itself are all worth looking at again and again, but it is the totality that really matters. None of it is expressly Scottish (there are hints, but hints only, of Mackintosh), and yet this is a place for presbyterian worship, a place for the preaching of the Word made flesh, and a place for singing Hebrew psalms, Scots Renaissance paraphrases, and the lush hymns of the Victorians. It is out of tune with how sections of the church see themselves today, but it challenges that view with another and perhaps deeper one.

156. *Chalmers Memorial Church of Scotland, Port Seton*

*T*his is another memorial church, but this time to a man who had a denominational rather than a personal connection with the building. Port Seton was a prosperous fishing village when this church was built for the United Free church, soon after the church's creation by the amalgamation of the Free and United Presbyterian churches. Thomas Chalmers was instrumental in the Disruption of the Church of Scotland in 1843, which resulted in the formation of the Free Church (see Kilmany, above, and the Introduction). This building, completed in about 1904, is a unique example of the 'Arts and Crafts' approach to church design. It has a tall saddleback tower with an ogee-roofed spire abutting a low church with dormer windows of a distinctly-domestic character, and most unusually with battered walls. The striking aisled nave has an open roof with stencilled decoration, a typical 'Arts and Crafts' feature, but here, dramatically executed in blue on cream, or cream on blue. There is a semicircular-vaulted chancel, containing the Communion table, with flanking open-loop tracery above the pulpit (left) and the choir seating (right). There is an aisle to the right (liturgical south) which has a central timber post round which the roof structure is arranged. The three stained-glass windows are by Margaret Kemp, Margaret Chilton and John Blyth. The architect was Sydney Mitchell, of Edinburgh (see also the Crichton Memorial Church, Dumfries, above). This is one of the most remarkable churches of a notably innovative period in church design in Scotland.

157. St John the Evangelist's Catholic Church, Portobello, Edinburgh

*A*nother example of the innovative approaches to design which followed the end of the nineteenth century, this church, designed by J. T. Walford and built between 1903 and 1906, has an extraordinary steeple, visible over a large area, with five tall octagonal turrets terminating in domed tops. The body of the church is more conventional, with late Scots Gothic tracery in the nave windows. There is an aisled nave and a semi-octagonal chancel, fashionable in the Roman Catholic churches of the time. There are carvings of angels at the tops of the columns in the nave arcades, and at the springing of the chancel arch. There are pitch-pine vaults over the clerestory windows, another feature fashionable in the early twentieth century. Most of the windows are glazed with leaded glass, with a stylised anthemion motif, but there is stained glass in the chancel windows. The west end of the north aisle is semi-octagonal, and was originally the baptistery. Its alabaster font has been brought forward into the chancel, and the space converted into a shop. The reredos has gone, but the altar has been repositioned in its original place, with a temporary wooden altar for post-Vatican II worship. The interior is darkly mysterious, but surprisingly conventional in comparison with the daringly innovative steeple. At the time when this church was built, on the site of two Georgian terrace houses, Portobello was both a fashionable outer suburb of Edinburgh, and a holiday resort.

158. St Margaret of Scotland's Scottish Episcopal Church, Braemar

Sir Ninian Comper has been mentioned in connection with St Andrew's Cathedral, Aberdeen, and St Mary's Church, Kirriemuir (see above), both built for the Scottish Episcopal Church. This is another of his buildings, built between 1899 and 1907. However, it is entirely different in character from St Andrew's and St Mary's. Externally, it is a uniquely-sensitive evocation of late Scots Gothic, with the juxtaposition of details from different places and traditions that makes the real Gothic so eternally fascinating. The church was built on a scale commensurate with the summer attendance by visitors. Externally, it is dominated by its great five-light east and west windows; in comparison, its squat, central, crenellated tower is relatively insignificant. The north transept was never built. Internally, the nave has a timber wagon roof, and the crossing is groin-vaulted in stone. The chancel has a coffered ceiling decorated with Tudor roses. There are choir stalls in English perpendicular style, and a lacy rood screen with a frieze of armorial bearings below the rood figures. The pulpit is bracketed out from the wall of the nave, and is reached by a spiral stair within the wall. It has a Gothic-panelled front, and a timber-vaulted and traceried canopy. Braemar is still a popular resort, but in the late nineteenth century it was a magnet for visitors who wished to take the chance of seeing royalty, as Queen Victoria and several of her family had estates in the area. The church also served several sporting estates at a time when the English upper classes migrated en masse in August to the Highlands for deer-stalking, grouse-shooting and salmon-fishing. Braemar still has something of the atmosphere of that period.

159. St Matthew's Church of the Nazarene, Paisley

Designed by W. D. McLennan, a Paisley architect and engineer, and built between 1905 and 1907, this is an example of the distortion for effect of traditional Gothic Revival. The 'west' and 'east' windows have been widened well beyond 'correct' proportions, and the tracery of the 'east' window is unmoulded, giving it a very chunky feeling. The railings and entrance towers have an Art Nouveau flavour, which would have been greatly enhanced had the proposed steeple been built. There is little externally to hint at the extraordinary character of the interior, which though it lacks the refinement of the work of Charles Rennie Mackintosh or J. Gaff Gillespie, Glasgow's leading exponents of the Art Nouveau, has a strength and masculinity absent from their work. The worship space, approached through a wide, low vestibule under the rear gallery, is a broad rectangle, with low side aisles acting as corridors. The large clerestory windows, like the 'west' window, are filled with leaded glass with McLennan's own tulip motif featuring largely. There are transepts, with galleries. The chancel, which is rather dark, contains Communion table, chairs and pulpit by McLennan, all, in dark-stained, straight-grained pine, like the gallery fronts. The pulpit has a 'crown of thorns' sounding board. The detailing is simple, the effect depending to a large extent on excellence in proportion. The nearest parallel to this interior is that of Eastbank (see above). St Matthew's is, however, much more original in its handling of space, if less concentrated in its detailed treatment. The building was constructed for a United Free congregation, soon after the union which created that Church, but is now owned by the Church of the Nazarene, a denomination with antecedents in Methodism, which took it over in 1988 and had restored it by 1992. The congregation was founded in 1909 in Orchard Street, nearby. St Matthew's was originally built as part of a major redevelopment of the surrounding part of central Paisley, with the construction of large new tenements to replace old weavers' houses, and with the widening of the main north-south road through the area to accommodate electric trams. It was a time when the town was prospering on the basis of its cotton sewing-thread mills, one of which, the Anchor Mills, is very close to the church.

160. *St Cuthbert's and South Beach Parish Church, Saltcoats*

This church is included as an example of Peter MacGregor Chalmers' masterly reinterpretations of the twelfth-century Romanesque to suit early twentieth-century expectations of both worship patterns and church design. It was completed in 1908. The aisled naves, arcades with thick cylindrical columns, small round-headed windows with cushion-headed capitals on plump nook shafts, and short semicircular-ended chancels are all recognisable from twelfth-century buildings, but MacGregor Chalmers used them in genuinely new ways. He used several different models for his towers. The St Cuthbert's tower is the most convincing of them all. All these Romanesque churches were built for the Church of Scotland, and were arranged for the Scoto-catholic form of worship fashionable at the time, with the Communion table at the end of the chancel, flanked by choir stalls, and with the pulpit at the left side of the junction of nave and chancel. This arrangement is well preserved in St Cuthbert's, the pulpit, table and font, of Chalmers' design, all being of exceptional quality. When this church was built, Saltcoats was both a seaside residential area and a holiday resort.

161. *Our Lady and St Meddan's Catholic Church, Troon*

*T*his extraordinary church, built in 1910–11, is a remarkably compelling synthesis of Scots Renaissance and 'Arts and Crafts' design, by Reginald Fairlie. It replaced the first Catholic church in Troon, St Patrick's, built on a different site in 1882–3. As with St Mary's Episcopal Church, Kirriemuir (see above), the massive tower (here in rock-faced masonry) is the key to the composition. The parapet is solid as at St Monans and its derivatives (see above), but the cope is decorated with figure sculpture. On the north side of the tower is a stair tower with an open-work crocketted spire, the delicacy of which interacts with the solidity of the tower in a most engaging way. The major openings in the building are round-headed in the manner of King's College Chapel, Aberdeen (see above), an example of the Romanesque revival of the early sixteenth century. The body of the church is powerfully buttressed, as at St Leonard's-in-the-Fields, Perth (see above). Internally, there is an aisled nave, with round-arched arcades. The nave roof is an open timber one, with carved angels projecting from the lower ends of the principal rafters. There is a short chancel, with a Lady Chapel to the left, and another chapel to the right. The chancel arch is pointed. There is a semi-octagonal apse, with a tripartite altarpiece, though the altar has been brought forward to the front of the chancel as prescribed by Vatican II. Carved wooden screens separate the chapels from the chancel, one with flamboyant unglazed tracery, the other with simple arcading. The ambo (pulpit) is panelled, with a band of panels carved in linenfold manner. The windows are all glazed with small-paned leaded glass, except for two windows in the vestibule. The organ is in a rear gallery inset into the tower. This bald, factual summary description can in no way begin to describe the exceptional quality of this interior. If the Pugin and Pugin churches (see St Patrick's Roman Catholic Church, Coatbridge, above) epitomise late nineteenth-century devotional Catholicism, this church has a lightness of touch that is definitely of the twentieth century. When it was built, Troon was expanding as the most prestigious seaside residential town on the Clyde, and a high-class holiday and golfing resort.

162. Hoselaw Chapel (Church of Scotland)

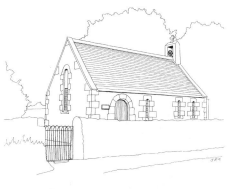

*A*fter all these great churches, products of wealth and symbols of power, this church is at the opposite extreme of scale and intention. This tiny Romanesque building with minute nave and minuscule round-ended chancel was built in about 1912 as a chapel of ease of the parish church of Linton, in upland Roxburghshire. So small that one can (and I did) miss it when driving past, it was designed for the farm servants of a remote area, but the care which Peter MacGregor Chalmers put into this little structure still shines through. Its scale is comparable with that of many of the small early-medieval chapels whose ruins can be found all over Scotland, and in entering this building one can, I believe, feel a sense of the worship for which these chapels were designed.

163. Lowson Memorial Church of Scotland, Forfar

*B*uilt to serve an expansion of Forfar to the east, this church was given by the family of a local linen manufacturer, James Lowson, in his memory. He had been a supporter of the project of building a Church of Scotland place of worship to serve the east end of the town. Designed by A. Marshall Mackenzie, Aberdeen, and opened in 1914, it uses late Scots Gothic motifs externally in a wholly original synthesis. The massive tower is here the centrepiece of a cruciform building.

There is a slender, octagonal tower on top of the spire, supported on a reinforced-concrete platform. The nave is aisled, with round-headed arches. The wood-lined ceiling has transverse 'vaults' to allow light to flood into the church from the four-light clerestory windows. Stained glass is confined to the east, west and transept windows, all designed by Douglas Strachan, as a unified group. The west window, depicting scenes from the Christian history of the district, lights the vestibule, which is separated from the nave by a screen supporting the organ and the choir seating. The exterior is pleasing, though the deliberate distortion of pre-Reformation proportion is initially vaguely disquieting. The interior is, however, entirely captivating. The calm, unusually light nave, with its simply-detailed arcades, leads one up to the darker crossing, transepts and chancel, where the flowing leadwork and richly-coloured glass of the windows, integrated across the mullions, take one's breath away. By any standards this is a remarkable work of art, as well as a most inspiring worship space. The area in which it is set has retained its middle-class residential atmosphere.

164. *Wallneuk North Church of Scotland, Paisley*

*L*owson Memorial was built with money made from textiles, and so, too, was Wallneuk North. Lowson Memorial is a landmark building in Forfar, and of the Scoto-catholic movement in the Church of Scotland; Wallneuk North is equally a landmark building in Paisley, and of the United Free Church, with its emphasis on preaching rather than on liturgy. Indeed, it was the largest church – and one of the last – built for that denomination before it united with the Church of Scotland in 1929. It was completed in 1915, initially as a daughter church of St James', to serve the north and east of the town, which in employment terms was dominated by the Anchor Mills of J. and P. Coats, the world's leading firm of sewing-thread manufacturers. The benefactor was Sir Peter Coats of that firm, and the architect was T. G. Abercrombie, Paisley's leading architect. Abercrombie, and probably his patron, chose to avoid the semi-barbaric richness of churches like Hippolyte Blanc's St James' and Thomas Coats Memorial churches in Paisley, and St Cuthbert's, Edinburgh; they also chose to avoid the layered meaning of the Arts and Crafts and Art Nouveau buildings mentioned immediately above, and the recreation of a vanished medieval culture, as was going on at Paisley Abbey at the time. Their approach to creating an appropriate space for worship instead emphasised dignity and relative simplicity. The exterior of the building, of red sandstone, is a carefully-integrated design, with the halls and other ancillary accommodation balancing the great mass of the main church building. The style is Abercrombie's own interpretation of English Perpendicular, with detailing to increase the vertical emphasis on the west front. Internally, the building is essentially on a T-plan, with a shallow apse accommodating the organ, installed in 1931 by Abbott and Smith, Leeds, in a case designed by Wylie and Lochead, Glasgow. The instrument is dedicated to the memory of Sir Peter Coats. There are galleries in both transepts, and at the back of the broad aisle-less nave. All the large windows are filled with cathedral glass, giving the space a bright, light feel, even in dull weather. But what is most striking about the interior is the remarkable sense of spaciousness and freedom from clutter. It is almost the apotheosis of the preaching church, but without stressing at all the function of the building as an auditorium. There is a grandeur about the handling of the space that reveals that Abercrombie was a masterly architect, one who could use tradition without being a slave to it. The First World War effectively put paid to the concept of grandeur in church design, and the experience of Wallneuk makes one realise what a loss that was – minor in relation to the totality of loss in that tragic conflict, but poignant nonetheless. The building dominates an area that has been fragmented by the piecemeal redevelopment which has characterised much of north Paisley since the 1960s.

165. St Ninian's Catholic Church, Gretna

*T*he village of Gretna was created during the First World War to house workers in a vast factory constructed to meet the insatiable demand for explosives created by the war. The housing was designed to be permanent, and community facilities were provided on an appropriate scale, including Church of Scotland, Episcopal and Roman Catholic churches. The last-named is by far the most striking and original one. It was designed by C. Evelyn Simmons, who was one of
the team of government architects responsible for creating Gretna, and it was completed in 1917. It is built of brick, in a stark and uncompromising manner, The style is Byzantine Romanesque, and the building is very tall in relation to its plan. The internal effect is

dramatic, with all the spaces finished with plaster vaults, contrasting with the roughness of the exposed brick walls and arch rings. The nave vault is pointed, and the chancel is a barrel vault. The crossing has a shallow dome, and there is a semicircular domed apse. The chancel is flanked by two small chapels, also domed. The chancel is simply furnished for post-Vatican II worship. The inherent strength of Romanesque design is amply shown in the compelling quality of this interior.

166. Old West Parish Church, Greenock

*P*erhaps this church should have been included much earlier, with those built in the late sixteenth century, for the original West Church was built in 1591, as a chapel of ease of the parish of Inverkip. It is said to have been the first church built in Scotland after the Reformation. It was originally rectangular, but was altered in about 1670, when the south, Schaw aisle was added, containing a burial vault with a laird's loft above, and with an external balustraded stair. A north aisle may well have been added at the same time, giving the church a Greek-cross plan (see Lauder above). The north aisle was probably the Communion aisle. The building was refaced in ashlar in 1864 by James Salmon. The original site, in what became Nicolson Street, was by the 1920s overshadowed by a shipbuilding yard which had been acquired during the First World War by Harland and Wolff of Belfast. When that company wished to expand its capacity immediately after the war, it acquired the church on the basis that it would be taken down and rebuilt on the present site using the original materials as far as possible, that a new tower would be built, and that a new church hall would be provided. The hall – known as the Pirrie Hall, after the chairman of Harland and Wolff – was built first, and used for worship while the translation of the church was undertaken. The relocation of the church was completed between 1926 and 1928, the architect for the whole project being James Miller. The building reads as a 1920s structure, rather than a sixteenth to seventeenth-century one, but photographic evidence strongly suggests that Miller's work was scholarly, and that the regularity of the masonry is really Salmon work. The rather dull tower is certainly, as agreed, Miller's. The Pirrie Hall is a very successful and appropriate new building, forming a courtyard with the south and east wings of the church. Internally, it looks as though the pre-1920s appearance of the building has effectively been recaptured. Even the burial aisle has been recreated, in brick, though there are no bodies in it. Many of the tombstones and monuments from the old churchyard have been relocated to an area to the west of the Pirrie Hall and the church, the mortal remains being re-interred in Greenock Cemetery. Opinions as to the virtue of relocation differ, but I think it was worthwhile from the church's point of view: the result was a very pleasing worship space and an excellent church hall. It was not so worthwhile from the Harland and Wolff perspective: the yard extension was not completed, and indeed the old yard closed in the 1930s.

167. *St Peter's Scottish Episcopal Church, Linlithgow*

On a much smaller scale than St Ninian's, Gretna, but also in Byzantine Romanesque, this church was built in 1928 as a memorial to George Walpole, Bishop of Edinburgh, and his wife Mildred, to designs by J. Walker Todd of Dick Peddie and Todd, Edinburgh. It is on a narrow site in the high street of Linlithgow, and because it is set back from the building line it is easy to miss when driving through the burgh. However, it should not be missed, for it is a gem, a beautiful miniature, with superb detailing. It has a central cupola, and there is a semicircular apse with a half-dome roof, to the rear.

168. *Reid Memorial Church of Scotland, Edinburgh*

One of the last churches in Scotland to be built of stone, and one of the largest inter-war churches, the Reid Memorial is on a striking site at the angle between West Savile Road and Blackford Avenue in Blackford, a southern suburb of Edinburgh. The architect was Leslie Grahame Thomson, and it was built between 1929 and 1933 in Arts and Crafts Gothic. The west window, above the main entrance, is set in a tall recess with a crocketed head, giving the west end a uniquely dramatic effect. The idiosyncratic treatment of the details is vaguely unsettling, but the composition is redeemed by the scale of the building and the way it exploits its site. The interior is set out for Scoto-catholic worship, with a pointed tunnel-vaulted chancel and barrel-vaulted nave. The woodwork is elaborately carved. The reredos incorporates a painting of Judas Iscariot being expelled from the Last Supper.

169. *Wilson Memorial United Free Church, Portobello, Edinburgh*

*T*he only 'Art Deco' church in Scotland, built in 1933 for a United Free congregation which stayed out of the union between that church and the Church of Scotland in 1929. It is brick-built and partly harled, in a manner common in the 1930s. It is distinguished by its tall tower, the centrepiece of its otherwise horizontally-disposed frontage. It was constructed to serve a growing area of middle-class housing.

170. *Catholic Church of the Immaculate Conception, Fort William*

*T*his is another Reginald Fairlie church (see Our Lady and St Meddan's, Troon, above) dominated by a massive tower. However, it is much more simply detailed than other Fairlie churches, and relies for its external impact on rough granite facing and the authority of the tower. It was built in a simplified Romanesque style. The tower has a solid parapet like that at St Monans Parish Church (see above), and has an external stair turret like that at Anstruther Easter Parish Church (see above). Behind the tower is a worship space dominated by a series of round-headed, reinforced-concrete portal frames, appropriately, as the church was built to serve immigrant workers in the new Lochaber Aluminium Works on the outskirts of the town. The portal frames give a strong rhythm to the nave and lead the eye to the chancel, in the base of the tower, which is framed by an explicitly Romanesque sandstone chancel arch. The tall chancel windows have late-Gothic tracery in their heads. There is a wrought-iron baldacchino in the chancel, with a pyramid-roofed canopy. The Lady Chapel is off the south side of the nave, and is approached through two round-headed arches carried on cylindrical columns with scalloped capitals. The contrast between the dark roughness of the exterior and the delicate elegance of the interior is challenging, but the lasting impression is of the thoughtfulness of this superb building.

171. *St Peter-in-Chains Catholic Church, Ardrossan*

Reginald Fairlie was unquestionably the best architect working for the Roman Catholic Church in Scotland in the early twentieth century. In the 1930s, however, Jack Coia of Gillespie, Kidd and Coia began to build some striking churches in the west of Scotland. The first of these was St Anne's Dennistoun, in Glasgow, completed in 1933. St Peter-in-Chains, opened in 1938, is on a traditional plan – a basilica, with a tower on the right-hand front corner – but the detailing is unusual and owes its inspiration to contemporary continental European practice. The tower is said to have been inspired by that of Stockholm Town Hall. As was common in the 1930s, for reasons of economy, the church is brick-built, but Coia made a virtue of this by using projecting bricks to vary the wall surface, and using radiating courses of thin bricks in the head of the west and south doors to give a lively, upward emphasis. The tower has an octagonal, flat-roofed, copper-clad top stage, an economical way to enhance the impression of modernity. The interior is simple but impressive. The rectangular windows in the aisles and clerestory have unusually-placed glazing bars, enlivening what would otherwise be a rather dull pattern of windows. The low aisles have plastered wagon roofs. The broad, shallow chancel has been altered to suit post-Vatican II worship, with the marble altar brought forward, but the scalloped canopy over the rear of the chancel has been retained The simple, almost Art Deco ambo has been relocated to the right of the chancel, its original position to the left being marked by a small curved canopy. The organ is in a rear gallery. The pews are unusually low-backed, and are beautifully proportioned. Though not as dramatic an interior as St Columba's, Hopehill Road, Glasgow (see below), or as intimate as St Anne's, Dennistoun, the calm simplicity here seems in complete harmony with the open seascape which greets the worshipper as he or she leaves the building.

172. *St Mary's Church of Scotland, King Street, Aberdeen*

*I*n contrast to St Peter-in-Chains, in St Mary's the architect, A. G. R. Mackenzie, with a similarly modernist intention, uses rough-hewn granite in small blocks, a series of flat roofs, and a complete absence of detailed modelling to create a soaring, stripped composition which still manages to evoke a sense of the essence of Gothic. The building was built between 1937 and 1939 to serve a new housing area. The masonry treatment and the massing of the tower are comparable with Reginald Fairlie's Church of the Immaculate Conception, Fort William (see above). The very tall, narrow windows in the west front may have been inspired by the similarly-proportioned ones on the west front of the nearby St Machar's Cathedral (see above).

173. *St Columba's Catholic Church, Glasgow*

*O*ne of the few churches completed during the Second World War (in 1941), this is a large brick-faced church, with a tiled roof sweeping down at the sides to low panelled walls. It was designed by Jack Coia, of Gillespie, Kidd and Coia. The west, entrance front is said to have been inspired by early Italian Romanesque churches in the Lucca area. It is monumental, consisting of a great vertical slab with an almost classical cornice, and pierced by an elongated cross-shaped window, which is flanked by inset panels with triple-arched heads. There is a triple doorway in a light-coloured stone, and the central doorway had vigorous high-relief sculpture in, above and below the tympanum, by Archibald Dawson, then head of sculpture at the Glasgow School of Art. The slab front is flanked by lower round-ended stair towers with Roman-tiled roofs in a distinctly Italian manner. It is, however, the interior of this church that is its great glory, with its rhythmic sequence of parabolic-arched, reinforced-concrete portal frames leading the eye forward to the focus of worship, a shallow sanctuary with a semi-octagonal apse. The use of portal frames echoes that in Reginald Fairlie's Church of the Immaculate Conception, Fort William (see above). Large windows at clerestory and aisle level between the portal frames ensure that the natural light shows off the frames to advantage. The sanctuary is flanked by the Sacred Heart and Lady chapels, to left and right. The concept is Gothic, but the planar faces of the portal frames give a unifying simplicity lacking in the Gothic apparatus of columns, arches and vaults. The narrow aisles, which function as corridors, have similar arches. The painted Stations of the Cross are the work of Hugh Adam Crawford, and were originally in the Catholic Pavilion (also designed by Jack Coia) at the Scottish Empire Exhibition held in Bellahouston Park in 1938. The sanctuary has been very successfully reordered to suit post-Vatican II worship. Modern banners and other hangings enhance the worship space in a sensitive way. The presbytery is to the south of the church, and is similarly, but more simply, detailed. When the church was built, the surrounding area was densely built up with tenements and industrial buildings. It has disintegrated in planning terms, with virtually all older buildings demolished, and piecemeal redevelopment. In this unpromising setting the church's architectural quality is particularly significant, and its recent repair is a gesture of faith in a place which needs it.

174. The Italian Chapel, Lamb Holm, Orkney

*A*unique and very moving building, constructed in 1943 by Italian prisoners of war drafted to Orkney to build the anti-submarine Churchill barriers linking the South Isles of Orkney to the Orkney mainland. The prisoners included several skilled craftsmen, who persuaded the British authorities to give them two corrugated-iron Nissen huts, placed end-to-end to convert into a church. Led by Domenico Chiochetti, they built an entrance front out of the reinforced concrete that was being used in vast quantities to build the barriers, and fitted out the interior using scrap materials. This bald description suggests something that, while ingenious, would look like a basic wartime 'put-past', and indeed that is the impression from the outside. What redeems it from that, however, is the interior, with its extraordinary painted decoration, much of it *trompe l'oeil*, which gives a remarkable sense of solidity and spaciousness. The effect is all the more striking both because the chapel is set in a typically-spare Orkney landscape, and because the inter-war period had seen a marked move away from elaboration in church decoration. In their conception of a worship space – a fitting setting for the sacrifice of the mass – this extraordinary group of Italians seem to have wiped out the Fascist period in Italian history, and the experiences of imprisonment and routine labouring. These were men whose love of God and of neighbour had triumphally survived the brutalising effects of Fascist materialism and of modern warfare. The space they created says more about the human – and the Holy – spirit than almost any other in Scotland.

175. *Colinton Mains Church of Scotland, Edinburgh*

*T*he post-war shortage of building materials and the wish to provide churches for new housing areas were in constant tension in the late 1940s and the 1950s. This encouraged the use of harled common brick for walling, a material which allowed Ian G. Lindsay and Partners, and others, to use as aesthetic inspiration the harled and whitewashed country churches in Caithness and in some Lowland counties, running counter to the post-war fashion for the International Modern Movement. In consequence, churches built in vernacular revival manner mode have been generally neglected by architectural commentators. Colinton Mains, built in 1954, is one such church. However, in my view it is a considerable aesthetic success, and stands up better as an architectural concept than the nearby, and almost contemporary, St John's, Oxgangs, an Alan Reiach Modern Movement building, much acclaimed at the time, with a design that now looks distinctly dated. Colinton Mains is on a T-plan, in eighteenth-century fashion. There is a west-end tower, with a slated spire terminating in a louvred cupola. The round-headed and circular windows are arranged in a manner reminiscent of Eccles Parish Church, Berwickshire. The interior is arranged with the pulpit, painted and fitted with a sounding board, in the centre of the south, long wall. Like St John's, St Hilda's Scottish Episcopal Church, and St Mark's Catholic Church, Colinton Mains was designed to serve a large area of new housing built on agricultural land in the mid-1950s to relieve overcrowding in central Edinburgh.

176. *St Paul's Catholic Church, Glenrothes*

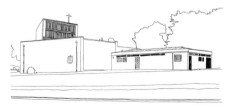

*G*lenrothes was established as a New Town in 1949, initially to house miners in what was intended to be a new 'super-pit', sunk by the National Coal Board to replace some of the older, inefficient Scottish pits. The new town needed new churches. The first, St

Margaret's Church of Scotland (1953–4), was mildly modern. In marked contrast to this, and to the Coia churches of the 1930s and 1940s (see St Peter-in-Chains, Ardrossan and St Columba's, Glasgow, above), St Paul's was the first complete break with tradition in post-war Scottish church design. The worship space is trapezoidal, with the entrance on the narrow side, so that the nave broadens towards the chancel, which is broad and shallow and lit primarily from a tall vertical roof-light illuminating the altar and giving it a prominence reflecting its liturgical significance. The asymmetric placing of a cross (on the axis of the centreline of the front range of the presbytery) on top of the rooflight emphasises the unorthodoxy of the design. The nave, chancel and presbytery are all flat-roofed, adding to the startling modernity, but posing problems with rainwater disposal (this problem also plagues other post-war churches). The interior is very plain, with white-painted brick walls. The only significant decorative detail is a wiry cross, 12 feet tall, set above the altar. This was designed by Benno Schotz, the leading sculptor in Scotland at the time. It incorporates abstracted references to events surrounding the Crucifixion. The design of this little building reflects the introduction to Gilllespie, Kidd and Coia of Isi Metzstein and Andy McMillan, who brought a refreshing modernity of thinking into the practice. The studio of Coia, Metzstein and McMillan produced what is unquestionably the finest group of post-war churches in Scotland (see below). St Paul's has been altered somewhat since the 1950s, and by virtue of the passage of time no longer looks startlingly modern. It still, however, appeals on account of its simplicity. The Rothes Colliery was not a success, but the town, now the headquarters of Fife Council, has prospered.

177. *St Bride's Catholic Church, East Kilbride*

East Kilbride was Scotland's first New Town, established in 1947. At first, the emphasis was on housing and industry, the intention being to resolve the post-war shortage of housing, and to broaden the west of Scotland's industrial base. Then came the first generation of new churches, all innovative to some extent, and then, in 1963–4, St Bride's, probably the most controversial of all Scotland's post-war churches. St Bride's carries the concept of roof lighting even further, and reintroduces the variation of brick walls used in some pre-war churches – including St

Peter-in-Chains, Ardrossan (see above) – but on a much larger scale. The sheer brick walls, rising from a mound, are at first sight distinctly fortress-like, rather like a pre-artillery castle of enclosure, and at the time of its completion the building was nicknamed 'Fort Apache'. It is, however, an immensely subtle building, and repays careful examination. As built, the church had a slender brick campanile in front of the presbytery, a contrast to the mass of the box-shaped brick church, but the campanile was taken down in the mid-1980s on the ground of structural instability. The interior is remarkable: a vast, flat-ceilinged space with light streaming in through roof lights, three of them projecting above the wallheads, and distinctively shaped. Most of the top lighting is diffused by timber slats, with secondary illumination from small windows in the 'north' wall of the nave. There is a concrete-framed side gallery, and facing it the pulpit is bracketed from the 'north' wall. The chancel is within the same rectangular plan as the 'nave', the altar having a concrete canopy, with a triple-arched under-surface. The entrance is contrived though a narrow slit on the 'south' face of the building, with a sinuous wall acting as a draught screen. The brick walls are neither rendered nor painted. This is a building that commands attention, even without its campanile. The presbytery, with its horizontal strip glazing, emphasises by contrast the height and bulk of the worship space.

178. St Patrick's Catholic Church, Kilsyth

*U*nlike Glenrothes and East Kilbride, Kilsyth is an old burgh, which expanded in the late nineteenth century to house coal miners, many of whom were Catholics. From the 1920s many of the families were rehoused in council houses, without significant change to the centre of the town. To find a major new church in a place like this is a surprise. Like St Bride's, St Patrick's Kilsyth was designed by Gillespie, Kidd and Coia and, more strongly than any of their other churches, shows the influence on the practice of Le Corbusier, the French architect whose chapel at Ronchamps, in eastern France was a seminal work. St Patrick's, completed in 1965, is much more geometric than Ronchamps, but has a similar edge profile to its flat roof. It is, in fact, the severe rectilinearity of St Patrick's, contrasting with the curved roof edge, that makes its design so compelling. The church replaced a small Gothic Revival building of the same name, opened in 1866, and is squeezed between existing buildings, with its entrance front partly obscured by the Victorian presbytery of the original St Patrick's. On this side the building has a semi-basement, incorporating a mortuary chapel and other auxiliary rooms. The roof of this space acts as the floor of a side gallery. The worship space is set across the building, and is lit by a band of glazing below the eaves, and by tall vertical windows on the south front, which faces a forecourt now used as a car park. The flat roof is steel-framed, and its curved edge is copper-clad. As in St Bride's, East Kilbride, the chancel area is part of the same rectangular-plan space as the seating area. The facing brick throughout is untreated. This is a much calmer building than St Bride's and a significantly simpler one. It does not have the presence in the community of the East Kilbride church, but is well worth seeking out.

179. Our Lady of Sorrows Catholic Church, Garrynamonie, South Uist

*T*he only Modern Movement church in the Outer Hebrides, this building was constructed in 1965 to serve the growing Catholic population of an island whose Catholicism had survived the Reformation. It was designed by Richard McCarron, of Edinburgh. The building is a distinguished example of its type, on a roughly triangular plan, with the layout focusing on the altar. The external treatment is strongly sculptural, with bold and well-composed use of advancing and receding vertical planes on its entrance front. It is set on the main north-south road on the island, overlooking the crofting township of Garrynamonie.

180. St Mungo's Church of Scotland, Cumbernauld

*C*umbernauld was, until the mid-1950s, a small village on the Glasgow to Stirling road, but like East Kilbride and Glenrothes it was designated a New Town. Its design took account of experience gained from building the earlier New Towns, and of the growing importance of motor transport. It was laid out with a central spine road, parallel subsidiary roads, and neighbourhoods where pedestrians and motor vehicles were segregated. In the geographical centre of the town as originally planned, a 'town centre' was built, with Scotland's first covered shopping mall. St Mungo's Church of Scotland was an integral part of the concept, linked to the complex by footpath. The new church was designed by Alan Reiach, Eric Hall and Partners of Edinburgh, expressly as a thoroughly modern building. It was completed in 1966. St Mungo's has a square worship space and, like St Patrick's, it has eaves-level glazing, but there the comparison ends, for St Mungo's has a truncated pyramidal copper roof, with a steeper-pitched, but matching belfry above low brick walls. Internally, the pulpit, Communion table and font are on a central platform, with ranks of pews on three sides, reviving the notion of central planning which was a feature of Burntisland (see above) and of some late eighteenth-century churches. The ceiling is of varnished wood. The impression on entering the building is of spaciousness, and plainness, very much in the Reformed tradition. To the west is a range of halls and other offices, forming an open, south-facing courtyard. The complex is reached from St Mungo's Road by a broad flight of steps, giving it additional dignity. The building does not evoke the fizzing excitement of the best churches from the Coia studio, but it has its own appeal, and makes a significant contribution to the character of the New Town.

181. *St Mary Magdalene Catholic Church, Edinburgh*

*S*t Mary Magdalene is, to my mind, one of the most purely sculptural of the 1960s churches. Unlike Our Lady of the Sorrows, South Uist (see above), where the external design is based on a series of parallel vertical planes, the treatment here involves planes angled to each other, with angled heads. Like Craigsbank (below), another sculptural building, it was designed by Rowand Anderson, Kininmonth and Paul, and was opened in 1966.

182. *Craigsbank Church of Scotland, Edinburgh*

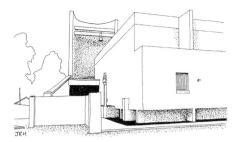

*F*ew churches evoke the innovative, experimental spirit of the 1960s better than Craigsbank, designed, like St Mary Magdalene, by Rowand Anderson, Kininmonth and Paul. The new church was added in 1964 and 1967 to an attractive but conservatively designed hall church built in 1937 to serve a large bungalow suburb of the village of Corstorphine. Externally, the treatment is strongly sculptural, in a much more explicit and obvious way than the Coia or Reiach and Hall building, with the cube housing the worship space raised on a plinth set back from its edges. To the west a curved screen wall embraces a bell, supported on a steel beam. The whole of the new building was originally unified by the white harl, a unity currently impaired by the patching which has followed partial failure of the harl. The drama of the exterior reflects the organisation of the worship space, which is square on plan, with steeply-raked pews on three sides and the chancel area on the fourth. A corridor runs right round the space, with the organ set in the middle of the east side. Natural lighting is from a clerestory. The layout of the worship space is intended to evoke the atmosphere of a conventicle, a Covenanting service held in the open air, in a natural amphitheatre. Appreciation of this exceptional building is hampered by its setting: it is tucked away at the end of a short street of the bungalows it was designed to serve, and hemmed in by suburban gardens. Externally, this church looks a little mannered now, but it is a strong design. The worship space is pleasingly simple and intimate.

183. *St Andrew's Catholic Church, Livingston*

*L*ivingston was Scotland's fourth New Town, and was set up in 1962. It incorporated several existing communities, but deliberately eschewed an obvious structure, making it a difficult place in which to navigate. The subduing of traditional planned structure makes the siting of places of worship equally difficult to follow (also a problem in the later phases of the development of Cumbernauld). This posed new challenges both to the organisation of the churches in Livingston, and also to the designers of church buildings. If rectilinearity was a common response by architects in search of a new church aesthetic in the 1960s, it was not the only one. Circular or near-circular and polygonal plans were also tried in new housing areas. Lochwood, Glasgow (now demolished), had a circular worship space, but though it worked well internally, it was somewhat sterile externally. Two near-circular churches designed by Alison, Hutchison and Partners are the best of these buildings. One is St Gabriel's, Prestonpans, in a traditional village, and the other is St Andrew's, Livingston, both for the Catholic Church. St Andrew's, opened in 1970, is much the more dramatic, with its perimeter wall designed as a series of over-lapping curves, the spaces between the ends of the curves forming slots for vertical glazing strips. The tops of the strips are also curved vertically, rising to a high point on the south side of the building, giving a sail-like effect, extraordinarily light and grace-ful. The interior is top-lit. This is beyond doubt the post-war church with the most dynamic exterior design of any in Scotland. It is also, arguably, the only new building in the New Town of any real architectural quality.

184. St Joseph's Catholic Church, Clydebank

*T*his church serves the Faifley housing estate, built in the early 1960s on the hills above Clydebank. The first church on this site was built in 1963, and was designed by Gillespie, Kidd and Coia. Its design was a modification of that of St Paul's, Glenrothes (see above), with a vertically-glazed roof-light illuminating the chancel area. The building was burned down in the mid-1990s and was replaced by the present structure, opened in 1997 and designed by Jacobsen and French, winners of an architectural competition. The Coia church was a definite statement in the landscape, but the Jacobsen and French building is lower. The worship space has an asymmetric rounded profile, made possible by the use of a metal-clad roof, light being from a clerestory on the east wall. It appears to nestle into the ground, and to shelter its people, a clear architec-tural expression of a trend in late twentieth-century Christian think-ing, that a vital role for the Church is to nurture people in their faith. This impression is reinforced by placing subsidiary buildings on either side of a paved forecourt, with a large timber free-standing cross in front. To my mind, this unassertive building is the best church, architecturally, built in Scotland in the last quarter of the twentieth century. Its interior, equally understated and designed specifically for post-Vatican II worship is light and welcoming. The curved, laminated timber beams supporting the roof are exposed, and the seating is arranged in gentle curves round the matching chancel steps. The altar and lectern are unassertive. An unusual feature is the baptistery, arranged for the option of adult baptism by immersion as well as infant baptism in the more conventional way.

List of churches with details of their locations

1. **Brechin Cathedral and Round Tower**, Church Lane, Brechin, Angus (NO595601)
2. **St Cuthbert's Parish Church**, Main Street, Dalmeny (West Lothian), City of Edinburgh (NT144775)
3. **St Mungo's Cathedral**, Castle Street, Glasgow (NS603656)
4. **St Magnus' Cathedral**, Broad Street, Kirkwall, Orkney Islands (HY449108)
5. **Dunfermline Abbey**, St Margaret Street, Dunfermline, Fife (NT090873)
6. **Symington Parish Church**, South Ayrshire (NS384314)
7. **Paisley Abbey**, Abbey Close, Paisley, Renfrewshire (NS486640)
8. **St Athernase's Parish Church**, Main Street, Leuchars, Fife (NT455214)
9. **Stobo Parish Church** (Stobo Kirk) (Peebles-shire), Scottish Borders (NT183377)
10. **Duddingston Parish Church**, Old Church Lane, Duddingston Village, Edinburgh (NT284726)
11. **St Blane's Cathedral**, The Cross, Dunblane (Perthshire), Stirling (NN782014)
12. **Culross Abbey Church**, Kirk Street, Culross, Fife (NS989863)
13. **St Ternan's Parish Church**, Arbuthnott (Kincardineshire), Aberdeenshire (NO801746)
14. **Cullen Old Kirk** (St Mary the Virgin's Parish Church), Cullen (Banffshire), Moray (NJ507664)
15. **Dornoch Cathedral**, High Street, Dornoch, (Sutherland), Highland (NH797897)
16. **St Machar's Cathedral**, The Chanonry, Old Aberdeen, City of Aberdeen (NJ939008)

17. **St Mary's Parish Church**, Sidegate, Haddington, East Lothian (NT519736)

18. **Dunkeld Cathedral**, Cathedral Street, Dunkeld (Perthshire), Perth and Kinross (NO024426)

19. **St Monans Parish Church**, Braehead, St Monans, Fife (NO523014)

20. **Holy Trinity Parish Church**, South Street, St Andrews, Fife (NO509167)

21. **St Michael's Parish Church**, Kirkgate, Linlithgow, West Lothian (NT002773)

22. **St John's Parish Church**, (St John's Kirk of Perth), St John Place, Perth, Perth and Kinross (NO119235)

23. **Fowlis Easter Parish Church**, City of Dundee (NO322334)

24. **St Matthew's Scottish Episcopal Chapel** (Rosslyn Chapel), Chapel Loan, Roslin, Midlothian (NT275631)

25. **Kilbirnie Old Parish Church** (Kilbirnie Auld Kirk), Dalry Road, Kilbirnie, North Ayrshire (NS315536)

26. **Corstorphine Old Parish Church**, Kirk Loan, Corstorphine, Edinburgh (NT201728)

27. **Steeple and Town Churches**, Nethergate, Dundee (NO401301-402301)

28. **High Church of St Giles** (St Giles' Cathedral), High Street, Edinburgh (NT257736)

29. **Church of the Holy Rude**, St John Street, Stirling (NS792937)

30. **King's College Chapel**, College Bounds, Old Aberdeen, City of Aberdeen (NJ940082)

31. **St Mary's Parish Church**, Ladykirk (Berwickshire), Scottish Borders (NT888477)

32. **Dunnet Parish Church** (Caithness), Highland (ND220712)

33. **Burntisland Parish Church**, East Leven Street, Burntisland, Fife (NT234857)

34. **St Quivox Parish Church**, Auchincruive, South Ayrshire (NS375241)

35. **Dirleton Parish Church** (Dirleton Kirk), East Lothian (NT513842)

36. **Cawdor Parish Church** (Nairnshire), Highland (NH843499)

37. **Greyfriars Tolbooth and Highland Kirk**, Greyfriars Place, Edinburgh (NT256734)

38. **Anstruther Parish Church**, Burial Brae, Anstruther Easter, Fife (NO567037)

39. **Kirkmaiden Parish Church** (Kirkmaiden Old Kirk) (Wigtownshire), Dumfries and Galloway (NX139324)

40. **Fenwick Parish Church**, Kirkton Road, Fenwick, East Ayrshire (NS465435)
41. **Lyne Parish Church** (Lyne Kirk) (Peebles-shire), Scottish Borders (NT192405)
42. **Ayr Old Parish Church** (The Auld Kirk of Ayr), off High Street, Ayr, South Ayrshire (NS339219)
43. **Lauder Old Parish Church**, Market Place, Lauder (Berwickshire), Scottish Borders (NT531475)
44. **Greenlaw Parish Church** (Berwickshire), Scottish Borders (NT712462)
45. **St Andrew's Parish Church**, Tongue (Sutherland), Highland (NC591570)
46. **Canongate Parish Church** (Canongate Kirk), Canongate, Edinburgh (NT265738)
47. **Durisdeer Parish Church** (Dumfriesshire), Dumfries and Galloway (NS894038)
48. **Yester Parish Church**, Main Street, Gifford, East Lothian (NT535681)
49. **Dalserf Parish Church**, South Lanarkshire (NS800507)
50. **St Andrew's Parish Church**, Main Street, Golspie, (Sutherland), Highland (NC837002)
51. **Hamilton Old Parish Church**, Strathmore Road, Hamilton, South Lanarkshire (NS723555)
52. **Kilmarnock Old High Parish Church**, Church Street and Soulis Street, Kilmarnock, East Ayrshire (NS430382)
53. **Crossmichael Parish Church** (Kirkcudbrightshire), Dumfries and Galloway (NX729669)
54. **Lunnasting Parish Church**, Lunna, Shetland Islands (HU486691)
55. **St Nicholas' Parish Church**, (Kirk of St Nicholas), Back Wynd, Union Street, Aberdeen (NJ941063)
56. **Mearns Parish Church**, Eagleham Road and Mearns Road, Newton Mearns, East Renfrewshire (NS551556)
57. **St Ninian's Catholic Chapel**, Mill of Tynet, Moray (NJ379613)
58. **Fogo Parish Church** (Berwickshire), Scottish Borders (NT931558)
59. **Oakshaw Trinity Church** (The High Kirk), Churchhill, Paisley, Renfrewshire (NS481642)
60. **Torphichen Parish Church**, The Bowyetts, West Lothian (NS969723)
61. **Wellpark Mid Kirk**, (Mid Kirk), Cathcart Square, Greenock, Inverclyde (NS740762)

62. **Inverness Old High Kirk**, Church Street, Inverness-shire, Highland (NH665455)
63. **Kilarrow Parish Church**, Bowmore, Isle of Islay, Argyll and Bute (NR312596)
64. **St Andrew's Parish Church**, King Street, Dundee (NO404307)
65. **Irvine Old Parish Church**, Kirkgate, North Ayrshire (NS322387)
66. **Dyke Parish Church**, Moray (NH990584)
67. **Kilmodan Parish Church**, Clachan of Glendaruel, Argyll and Bute (NR995842)
68. **St Andrew's and St George's Parish Church**, George Street, Edinburgh (NT255741)
69. **Kilmany Parish Church**, Fife (NO388218)
70. **Killean and Kilchenzie Parish Church**, A'Chleit, Argyll and Bute (NR681418)
71. **St Magnus' Parish Church**, Tingwall, Shetland Islands (HU419437)
72. **Annan Old Parish Church**, High Street, Annan (Dumfriesshire), Dumfries and Galloway (NY192666)
73. **Montrose Old and St Andrew's Parish Church** (Montrose Old), High Street, Montrose, Angus (N0715778)
74. **Catrine Parish Church**, Chapel Brae, Catrine, East Ayrshire (NS528260)
75. **St Fergus' Parish Church**, Kirk Wynd, Glamis, Angus (NO386469)
76. **Glenaray and Inveraray Parish Church**, Church Square, Inveraray, Argyll and Bute (NN096084)
77. **Baldernock Parish Church**, East Dunbartonshire (NS577751)
78. **Bellie Parish Church**, The Square, Fochabers, Moray (NJ345587)
79. **Highland Parish Church**, New Quay Street, Campbeltown, Argyll and Bute (NR720201)
80. **Echt Parish Church**, Aberdeenshire (NJ739057)
81. **Saltoun Parish Church**, East Saltoun, East Lothian (NT474678)
82. **Bourtie Parish Church**, Kirkton of Bourtie, Aberdeenshire (NJ804248)
83. **St Michael's Parish Church**, Inveresk, Musselburgh, East Lothian (NT344721)
84. **Peterhead Old Parish Church**, Aberdeenshire (NK131462)
85. **St George's Tron Parish Church**, Buchanan Street, Glasgow (NS590665)

86. **Glenorchy Parish Church**, Dalmally, Argyll and Bute (NN168275)
87. **Muirkirk Parish Church**, East Ayrshire (NS701278)
88. **Collace Parish Church**, Kinrossie (Perthshire), Perth and Kinross (N0197320)
89. **Nicolson Square Methodist Church**, Nicolson Square, Edinburgh (NT261732)
90. **North Leith Parish Church**, Madeira Street, Leith, Edinburgh (NT265765)
91. **St Andrew's Catholic Cathedral**, Clyde Street, Glasgow (NS592647)
92. **St Andrew's Scottish Episcopal Cathedral**, King Street, Aberdeen (NJ945065)
93. **Channelkirk Parish Church** (Berwickshire), Scottish Borders (NT481545)
94. **St Mungo's Parish Church**, Bedford Place, Alloa, Clackmannan (NS886929)
95. **St John the Evangelist's Scottish Episcopal Church**, Princes Street, Edinburgh (NT247736)
96. **Kirk o'Shotts**, near Salsburgh, North Lanarkshire (NS843629)
97. **Dunfermline Abbey Church**, St Margaret Street, Dunfermline, Fife (NT090873)
98. **Broughton St Mary's Parish Church**, Bellevue Crescent, Edinburgh (NT265748)
99. **Ettrick Parish Church** (Selkirkshire), Scottish Borders (NT260145)
100. **Lecropt Parish Church** (Perthshire), Stirling (NS781979)
101. **Limekilns Parish Church**, Church Street, Limekilns, Fife (NT781979)
102. **Croick Parish Church**, Ardgay (Ross and Cromarty), Highland (NH457915)
103. **Cortachy Parish Church**, Angus (NO396597)
104. **St Stephen's Church Centre**, St Vincent Street, Edinburgh (NT250746)
105. **St Giles' Parish Church**, High Street, Elgin, Moray (NJ216628)
106. **St Serf's Parish Church**, Tillicoultry, Clackmannan (NS973968)
107. **Portmoak Parish Church**, Scotlandwell (Kinross-shire), Perth and Kinross (NO183019)
108. **Bothwell Parish Church**, Main Street, Bothwell, South Lanarkshire (NS705586)

109. **Gordon Scottish Episcopal Chapel,** Castle Street, Fochabers, Moray (NJ346589)
110. **St Margaret's Catholic Church,** Chapel Street, Huntly, Aberdeenshire (NJ528409)
111. **St Mark's Unitarian Church,** Castle Terrace, Edinburgh (NT247735)
112. **Ardchattan Parish Church,** Achnaba, Argyll and Bute (NM945360)
113. **St Peter's Free Church,** St Peter Street, Dundee (NO390298)
114. **St Mary's Catholic Church,** Huntly Street, Inverness (Inverness-shire), Highland (NH662455)
115. **St Cuthbert's Parish Church,** St Mary Street, Kirkcudbright (Kirkcudbrightshire), Dumfries and Galloway (NX683509)
116. **St Margaret's Catholic Church,** Hallcraig Street, Airdrie, North Lanarkshire (NS765656)
117. **Alyth Parish Church,** Kirk Brae, Alyth (Perthshire), Perth and Kinross (NO243488)
118. **St Andrew's Parish Church** (Gartsherrie Church), Coatbridge, North Lanarkshire (NS733654)
119. **Penninghame St John's Parish Church,** Church Street, Newton Stewart (Wigtownshire), Dumfries and Galloway (NX410654)
120. **St Luke's Parish Church** (Old Church), Nelson Street, Greenock, Inverclyde (NS273763)
121. **St Ninian's Scottish Episcopal Cathedral,** North Methven Street Perth, Perth and Kinross (NO116237)
122. **Scottish Episcopal Cathedral of the Isles,** College Street, Millport, Isle of Cumbrae, North Ayrshire (NS165561)
123. **Renfield St Stephen's Church of Scotland,** Bath Street, Glasgow (NS582659)
124. **St Vincent Street and Milton Free Church,** St Vincent Street, Glasgow (NS583656)
125. **Renfrew Old Parish Church,** High Street, Renfrewshire (NS509676)
126. **Barclay Church of Scotland,** Bruntsfield Place, Edinburgh (NT249726)
127. **Catholic Church of the Immaculate Conception,** High Street, Lochee, Dundee (NO380314)
128. **Innerleithen Parish Church,** Leithen Road, Innerleithen, (Peeblesshire), Scottish Borders (NT332369)
129. **St Andrew's Scottish Episcopal Church,** Belmont Place, Kelso (Roxburghshire), Scottish Borders (NT728337)

130. **St Andrew's Scottish Episcopal Cathedral**, Ardross Street, Inverness (Inverness-shire), Highland (NH664450)
131. **Dingwall Free Church** (Ross and Cromarty), High Street, Highland (NH553587)
132. **Dysart Parish Church**, West Port, Dysart, Fife (NT303932)
133. **Palmerston Place Church of Scotland**, Palmerston Place, Edinburgh (NT241734)
134. **Queen's Park Baptist Church** (Camphill Queens Park), Balvicar Drive, Glasgow (NS578554)
135. **Kelvinside Hillhead Parish Church**, Saltoun Street and Observatory Road, Glasgow (NS567673)
136. **St John's Church of Scotland**, Argyll Street, Dunoon, Argyll and Bute (NS172769)
137. **St Mary's Scottish Episcopal Cathedral**, Palmerston Place, Edinburgh (NT257736)
138. **Priestfield Church of Scotland**, Dalkeith Road, Edinburgh (NT271721)
139. **Barony Church**, Dalswinton (Dumfriesshire), Dumfries and Galloway (NX942850)
140. **Galashiels Old Parish Church and St Paul's**, Scott Crescent, Galashiels (Selkirkshire), Scottish Borders (NT490362)
141. **Wellington Church of Scotland**, University Avenue, Glasgow (NS570667)
142. **St Andrew's Parish Church**, Churchgate, Moffat (Dumfriesshire), Dumfries and Galloway (NT075051)
143. **St Leonard's-in-the-Fields and Trinity Parish Church**, Marshall Place, Perth (Perthshire), Perth and Kinross (NO117232)
144. **St Sophia's Catholic Church**, Bentinck Street, Galston, East Ayrshire (NS504365)
145. **St Molio's Church of Scotland**, Shiskine, Isle of Arran, North Ayrshire (NR910295)
146. **Southwick Church of Scotland**, Caulkerbush (Kirkcudbrightshire), Dumfries and Galloway (NX906569)
147. **St Cuthbert's Parish Church**, Lothian Road, Edinburgh (NT248736)
148. **Thomas Coats Memorial Baptist Church**, High Street, Paisley, Renfrewshire (NS478640)
149. **St Patrick's Catholic Church**, Main Street, Coatbridge, North Lanarkshire (NS733651)
150. **Crichton Memorial Church**, The Crichton, Dumfries (Dumfriesshire), Dumfries and Galloway (NY983742)

151. **Cranshaws Parish Church** (Berwickshire), Scottish Borders (NT692618)
152. **Gardner Memorial Church of Scotland**, St Ninian's Square and Damacre Road, Brechin, Angus (NO600602)
153. **Greyfriars John Knox Church of Scotland**, Broad Street, Aberdeen (NJ943044)
154. **St Mary's Scottish Episcopal Church**, West Hillbank, Kirriemuir, Angus (NO383544)
155. **Eastbank Church of Scotland**, Old Shettleston Road, Glasgow (NS647643)
156. **Chalmers Memorial Church of Scotland**, Edinburgh Road, Port Seton, East Lothian (NT403747)
157. **St John the Evangelist's Catholic Church**, Brighton Place, Portobello, Edinburgh (NT304737)
158. **St Margaret of Scotland's Scottish Episcopal Church**, Braemar (Aberdeenshire), Aberdeenshire (NO153914)
159. **St Matthew's Church of the Nazarene**, Gordon Street, Paisley, Renfrewshire (NS485637)
160. **St Cuthbert's and South Beach Parish Church**, Caledonia Road, Saltcoats, North Ayrshire (NS244418)
161. **Our Lady and St Meddan's Catholic Church**, Cessnock Road, Troon, South Ayrshire (NS327311)
162. **Hoselaw Chapel** (Church of Scotland), near Morebattle (Roxburghshire), Scottish Borders (NT802318)
163. **Lowson Memorial Church of Scotland**, Jameson Street, Forfar, Angus (NO464509)
164. **Wallneuk North Church of Scotland**, Abercorn Street, Paisley, Renfrewshire (NS486643)
165. **St Ninian's Catholic Church**, Gretna (Dumfriesshire), Dumfries and Galloway (NY317674)
166. **Old West Parish Church**, Esplanade, Greenock, Inverclyde (NS279765)
167. **St Peter's Scottish Episcopal Church**, High Street, Linlithgow, West Lothian (NS000770)
168. **Reid Memorial Church of Scotland**, West Savile Terrace, Blackford, Edinburgh (NT261710)
169. **Wilson Memorial United Free Church**, Portobello Road, Edinburgh (NT296741)
170. **Catholic Church of the Immaculate Conception**, Belford Road, Fort William (Inverness-shire), Highland (NN107741)
171. **St Peter-in-Chains Catholic Church**, South Crescent, Ardrossan, North Ayrshire (NS233421)

172. **St Mary's Church of Scotland,** King St, Aberdeen (NJ943082)
173. **St Columba's Catholic Church,** Hopehill Road, Glasgow (NS583671)
174. **Italian Chapel,** Lamb Holm, Orkney (HY488006)
175. **Colinton Mains Church of Scotland,** Oxgangs Road North, Edinburgh (NT234693)
176. **St Paul's Catholic Church,** Warout Road, Glenrothes, Fife (NO281005)
177. **St Bride's Catholic Church,** Whitemoss Avenue, East Kilbride, South Lanarkshire (NS641544)
178. **St Patrick's Catholic Church,** Low Craigends, Kilsyth (Stirlingshire), North Lanarkshire (NS720777)
179. **Our Lady of Sorrows Catholic Church,** Garrynamonie, South Uist, Western Isles (NF759164)
180. **St Mungo's Parish Church,** Cumbernauld (Dunbartonshire), North Lanarkshire (NS757745)
181. **St Mary Magdalene Catholic Church,** Bingham Avenue, Bingham, Edinburgh (NT302725)
182. **Craigsbank Church of Scotland,** Craig's Bank, Corstorphine, Edinburgh (NT192731)
183. **St Andrew's Catholic Church,** Craigshill Road, Livingston, West Lothian (NT063680)
184. **St Joseph's Catholic Church,** Faifley Road, Clydebank, West Dunbartonshire (NS510733)

Select bibliography

There is an enormous volume of published material about Scottish churches, both as buildings and as denominations. Much of this is variable in quality, but none of it is negligible: people writing about their own building or belief do so from a sense of love, or loyalty, or both, and are always worth reading. This very select and summary list of books is of ones that I have found of particular value over the years. I have also read many of the guidebooks and leaflets produced by individual churches, and have consulted general topographical works of reference.

The *Buildings of Scotland* series of architectural guides

The *Royal Incorporation of Architects in Scotland*'s series of guides

Glendinning, Miles, Ranald MacInnes and Aonghus MacKechnie, *A History of Scottish Architecture*, Edinburgh: Edinburgh University Press, 1996.

Hay, George, *The Architecture of Scottish Post-Reformation Churches, 1560–1843*, Oxford: Oxford University Press, 1957.

Macgibbon, David and Thomas Ross, *The Ecclesiastical Architecture of Scotland from the earliest Christian Times to the seventeenth century* (3 volumes), Edinburgh: David Douglas, 1896–7.

The Scotland's Churches Scheme yearbooks, *Churches to visit in Scotland*, of which the most recent is the 2004 edition

Glossary

Aisle: used in two senses in this book. Firstly, it is a space parallel to the **nave** or **choir,** and to one side, separated by an **arcade** or by a partition with openings from the adjacent space. Secondly, it is an arm projecting from the body of a church, often containing a burial vault or a private gallery.

Ambulatory: a passage round the perimeter of a worship space designed to allow visitors to walk round a church without interfering with services in the inner space.

Apse: a projection from the end of a choir or aisles, often semicircular or polygonal on plan, usually designed to house an altar or Communion table.

Arcade: a row of arches.

Art Deco: a style of building and decoration popular between the two World Wars, characterised by stark geometric forms.

Arts and Crafts: a style popular in the late nineteenth and early twentieth century, using motifs and building techniques from traditional English (and, more rarely, Scottish) buildings.

Astragals: the horizontal and vertical wooden or metal divisions between the panes of glass in a window.

Baldacchino: a free-standing canopy, usually on four columns, over a specially-important object or place.

Baptistery: a part of a church set aside for the sacrament of baptism, and containing a font for that purpose. In presbyterian churches, and in modern Catholic worship, the font is usually in the chancel, not in a separate space.

Barrel vault: a form of **vault** which consists of a simple arched structure, usually semicircular, but occasionally pointed. The surface of the vault may be decorated by ribs, but these have no structural purpose.

Basilican: referring to a plan typical of early churches in the Roman empire, with a **nave** with **aisles** and an aisle-less **choir**.

Bellcote: another name for a belfry.

Blind: of **arcades** or **colonnades** which have a solid background.

Box pews: pews which have doors. The seating can either be along the back of the enclosure so formed, or may be all round the enclosure, sometimes with a central table. Such pews were popular in the eighteenth and early nineteenth century, as they were reasonably draught-proof.

Broach: of a spire, refers to one where the base is square, tapering to an octagonal plan. with sloping triangular faces at the corners.

Burgage plot: in a medieval burgh, a strip of land at right angles to the main street, with the house on the street frontage, and garden ground behind, tenanted or owned by a burgess of the burgh, a merchant or tradesman with rights to ply for business in the town.

Burial chapel or aisle: after the Reformation the Church of Scotland prohibited burial under the floors of churches. Some landowners then built annexes to existing churches which incorporated vaults for the accommodation of lead coffins. These are burial chapels or aisles.

Buttress: a substantial stone projection from the outside of a building designed to strengthen the wall so as to support the roof (either vaulted or timber).

Cap house: a projecting cover for the top of a spiral stair, where it reaches the top of a tower.

Cape Dutch: a style developed by Dutch settlers in southern Africa, characterised by gables with curved profiles, modified from sixteenth to seventeenth-century Dutch buildings.

Castellated: used to describe the treatment of a wall-head with alternate projections and spaces, originally devised for castles, to provide protection for the defenders, but popular in church building in the early nineteenth century.

Catholic Apostolic Church: an unusual and complex denomination which arose out of the charismatic experiences of a group of Scots living in London in 1830. It was governed by twelve 'apostles', and developed an elaborate hierarchy and liturgy, building some remarkably ornate churches, of which one survives, in secular use, in Edinburgh. The denomination died out after 1901, when the last 'apostle' died.

Chancel: another name for the **choir** of a church, but also used for an area at the front of a church set out with pulpit, Communion table or altar, and font, and providing a focus for worship.

Chapel, chapel of ease: a chapel can be a subsidiary part of a church, as in the Lady, Blessed Sacrament and Saints' chapels in a Catholic or episcopal church, and in many presbyterian churches, a space for meditation or for small services. Alternatively, it can be a separate building. Technically, any Christian place of worship in a Church of Scotland parish, other than the parish church, is a 'chapel' – hence the tradition of referring to Catholic churches as 'chapels'. This usage has fallen into decay, as has the concept of the 'chapel of ease', a place of worship, other than the parish church, provided for the convenience of worshippers, and without a Kirk Session of its own.

Chapter house: a room attached to an abbey or cathedral for the monks or priests to gather for business, and, in the case of abbeys, to hear a chapter of the regulations for the conduct of the abbey read by one of the monks.

Chevron: a form of decoration of a round-headed arch in **Romanesque** buildings characterised by zig-zag tooling on the face, and a saw-tooth profile for the underside of the arch ring.

Choir: a term used for the eastmost part of a two-compartment or **cruciform** church. In an abbey it is known as a presbytery – a place for the priests. Choirs were fitted with inward-facing stalls for the accommodation of the monks or clergy, and more recently of lay singers. See also **chancel.**

Clearances: used to describe the voluntary or compulsory removal by landowners of people from inland areas in the Highlands and Islands in the nineteenth century, to make way for sheep farming or for deer forests.

Clerestory: a row of windows high up in the wall of a church, usually in Gothic or Romanesque churches above the **arcades,** but in modern buildings simply high-level glazing.

Cluniac: refers to an abbey using the rule of monastic life developed in the French abbey of Cluny as a reformed version of the Benedictine order.

Collegiate: of late medieval churches, buildings served by groups of priests, and officially recognised by the administration of the Church as such.

Colonnade: a row of columns, the classical equivalent of an **arcade.**

Columban: relating to the form of worship and church organisation developed in Iona by St Columba and his followers.

Commonwealth: here used of the period when Scotland had a joint parliament with England, under Oliver Cromwell, in the 1650s.

Communion aisle: a part of a church specifically used for

Communion services. It was generally a projection from the main worship space, either at one end, or in a separate wing.

Confessionals: small rooms for priests to hear parishioners confessing their sins, and for the conferring of the sacrament of absolution by the priests. A partition separated penitent and clergyman, to assure anonymity. This practice is now obsolete in the Catholic Church, replaced by the sacrament of reconciliation.

Conventual: refers to the buildings used by religious communities, other than their churches.

Corbel table: the top course of stone in a **Romanesque** building, with projecting stones – corbels – to support the edge of the roof. The corbels are often carved with masks of human faces, with animals and birds, and with abstract designs.

Corinthian, Corinthianesque: of columns with capitals carved to resemble acanthus leaves, the most elaborate of classical columns. Greeks and Romans used slightly different forms and proportions. Corinthianesque is used of columns which do not copy, with reasonable accuracy, the details and proportions of classical models.

Credence: a shelf on which the bread and wine to be used in the Eucharist were placed before consecration.

Crockets: carved ornaments in the forms of stylised leaves, used to decorate the angles of spires and pinnacles, and sometimes as low-relief carvings round doors and windows.

Crossing: in a **cruciform** church, the space where the nave and choir intersect the line of the transepts. In some instances one or more limbs of the church have not been completed, but the term is still used for the central space.

Crown steeple: a way of terminating a tower, with arches curving in from the corners, and the mid-points of the sides, to a central point, as in a royal crown of the so-called 'imperial' type. The original crown steeples were in churches associated with the Stewart monarchs, but there are also revival versions.

Cruciform: of buildings on a cross plan, generally based on a Latin cross, with the nave longer than the other arms, but occasionally on a **Greek cross**.

Curvilinear tracery: late Gothic tracery, where the glazed area of the upper part of a window is split up by masonry strips in sinuous patterns.

Cushion-headed: of the capitals of some **Romanesque** columns, which have convex carving resembling cushioned upholstery.

Cusp: a feature of Gothic tracery, consisting of a projection with concave sides, almost universal until the sixteenth century.

Domical: of a dome-shaped form which has sides curved in two dimensions only, like a curved piece of paper.

Doric: the simplest form of classical column. Greek Doric columns are generally fluted, and squatter than **Corinthian** or Ionic columns. Roman Doric columns are slender.

Ecclesiological movement: a strand of thinking in the Anglican churches (including the Scottish Episcopal Church), the Catholic Church and the Church of Scotland which saw merit in returning to a more liturgical approach to worship, and to the laying-out of church buildings in a manner reflecting pre-Reformation thinking. The terms Oxford Movement and Tractarian Movement have similar meanings. See also **Scoto-catholic.**

Fan vaulting: a late Gothic style of vaulting developed in England, where the roof is formed by a series of slender ribs radiating from the tops of the supporting piers. and by the downward continuation of these ribs to make concave-sided central projections.

Finial: a free-standing vertical feature on top of a tower, buttress or wall-head, to give an effective visual stop. See also **pinnacle.**

Flamboyant: an equivalent term to **curvilinear,** referring to the flame-like elements in the tracery.

Frieze: in classical architecture, a flat band in the stonework (entablature) above columns. The frieze can either be plain, or decorated with sculpture, or with incised lettering.

Geometric tracery: a style of window treatment in middle-period Gothic, where the stone strips dividing up the glazed areas are in simple curved forms – circles, arches, and lobed shapes, formed by **cusps.** Geometric tracery was a favourite of Gothic revival architects, as machines could be used to generate the curved elements.

Gibbs-surround: a manner of treating the margins of windows and doors, devised by James Gibbs, with boldly-projecting blocks of stones alternating with shallower and narrower moulded ones. Applied to features on a plain wall, this proved a very effective detail.

Glasgow style: a loose term for the style of Charles Rennie Mackintosh, J. Gaff Gillespie and other turn-of-the-century architects who were conscious of Art Nouveau, but who used a more geometric approach.

Gothic survival: used to describe features of Gothic style carried on by post-Reformation craftsmen without any obvious break from their early-modern precursors.

Gothick: a term used to define buildings in which pointed windows feature, but in which the detailing bears no resemblance to 'real' Gothic. In a typical Gothick building in Scotland, the windows will be close to the outer face of the walls, and are likely to have timber **intersecting-arc** glazing.

Greek cross: an equal-armed cross (see **cruciform**).

Groined vault: a vault in the simplest form of which a cross arch intersects at right angles a longitudinal arch. In a polygonal apse, for example, much more complex forms occur.

Hammer-beam roof: an elaborate type of roof, in which the hammer beams project at right angles to the wall-heads, being supported at their inner ends by curved braces springing from corbels set in the walls. Uprights from the inner ends of the hammer beams support the rafters, and a crossbeam (collar), linking the rafters. An upright from the collar runs up to the apex of the roof, and curved braces run down to the ends of the hammer beams. This system allows fairly short pieces of timber to build a roof capable of spanning a broad space, but it is also distinctly ornamental, and sometimes used for that purpose.

Harled: of a wall, covered with a wet mixture of lime, sand and fine gravel which when dry gives a slightly rough surface. Harling is primarily used to waterproof walls.

Heritors: the owners of the land (heritable property) in a parish, responsible for church buildings in the Church of Scotland, for the payment of stipend to ministers, and (generally speaking) for the appointment of ministers (patronage) until 1870. The heritors were the owners of Church of Scotland church buildings until 1925, when they were transferred to the General Trustees.

Intersecting-arc tracery: as the name suggests, a style of tracery in which the stone strips (or later wooden astragals) forming the glazing divisions in the upper parts of windows are laid out as simple curves, creating a pattern of curved diamonds. This is, in stone, a sixteenth- and seventeenth-century style, and in timber a late eighteenth- and early nineteenth-century one (see **Gothick**). It is also found in some revival buildings.

Lay brothers: in some orders of monks, men who were in holy orders, but not ordained as priests, who engaged during the day in secular activities connected with the running of the monastery.

Loft: an old name for a gallery, often still applied to a private gallery used by a landowner.

Lombardic: referring to the province of Lombardy in what is now Italy, where the **Romanesque** style was developed as an all-over treatment for show fronts of churches. In Scotland it was used by revival architects as a visually-effective alternative to Gothic Revival.

Loop tracery: an equivalent term to **curvilinear** and **flamboyant.**

Lugged doorway: a treatment, characteristic of the late seventeenth and early eighteenth century, in which the top parts of the sides of the opening are extended to form short projections or lugs (ears).

Lunette: a half-moon-shaped window.

Lutheranism: the earliest form of institutional north-European protestantism, named after Martin Luther, its founder. It was influential in the early post-Reformation period in Scotland, and, I would argue, on the shape of seventeenth-century Scottish episcopalianism.

Mural monument: a monument built into, or onto, a wall. Earlier monuments usually took the form of tomb recesses with arched heads, often over **recumbent effigies.** In the late sixteenth and seventeenth centuries, elaborate monuments standing proud of the walls became popular among the very wealthy. Later monuments are generally more two-dimensional.

Narthex: a name for a space through which one passes from the outside world into the **nave** of a church. Generally, such spaces would now be termed vestibules or, more recently, welcome areas.

Nave: the main body of a church, in which the laity would assemble for worship. In an abbey church, where there were lay brothers, the space also accommodated the 'lay brothers' choir, partitioned off from the space for the laity.

Nissen hut: a temporary hut made by bolting together curved sections of corrugated iron to form a part-cylindrical shell, sitting on a concrete base, with brick, concrete or wooden ends. Called after its inventor, Lt Col. Peter Nissen, a British engineer.

Nook shafts: the shafts of columns set into the edges of windows, doorways or piers, with bases and capitals forming part of the main fabric of the building.

Obelisk: a vertical feature, of Egyptian origin, consisting of a tapering four-sided pillar with a pyramidal top, sometimes used as a **finial,** but more commonly as a free-standing monument.

Oversailing eaves: used to describe a building in which the roof overhangs the wall-head. A feature of **Arts and Crafts** buildings.

Perpendicular: a term used to describe late English Gothic, with large windows, often with flattened heads, divided into many lights by slender stone strips (vertical mullions and horizontal transoms). There is a Scottish equivalent, but it is not common, and less exaggerated. English Perpendicular, in its less extreme forms, was used in both early and late Gothic Revival in Scotland.

Pinnacle: almost an equivalent term to finial, but also used to describe small spires, especially in early Gothic Revival buildings.

Plate tracery: a form of window head in which the glazing pattern is carved out of what still read as flat pieces of stone.

Preceptory: simply the name given to the headquarters of the Knights Hospitallers of the Order of St John of Jerusalem.

Pulpitum: a massive stone screen separating the nave from the choir in an abbey church or cathedral.

Recumbent effigy: a feature of later pre-Reformation mural monuments, with high-relief sculptures of the deceased, lying on their backs.

Reredos: originally an ornamented backing to an altar, intended to give it dignity, and often incorporating painted or carved devotional images. In **Scoto-catholic** churches a reredos was often placed behind the Communion table in the chancel.

Retiring room: Where a landowner had a private **loft**, a retiring room was sometimes provided behind the loft, with sanitary facilities, and also a place where refreshments could be taken between or after services. As church buildings were often at a distance from heritors' residences, this was a useful concept in the days of horse transport.

Rococo: an exuberant style popular in central and southern Europe in the early eighteenth century, in which the disciplined ornament of the Baroque period was freed from restraint to give a richer feeling.

Romanesque: a term used to describe architecture in which small round-headed arches are used on external walls. Some writers distinguish an 'early British' style, but for simplicity I have conflated the two. The original Romanesque in Scotland is of the twelfth and early thirteenth centuries, and there were several revivals, referred to in the summary essay at the beginning of this book.

Rood screen: a wooden or stone screen between the choir and nave, through which the laity could see – partially – the ritual going on in the choir. The term derives from the figures of Christ on the cross, flanked by smaller figures of the thieves who were crucified with him, which were placed on the top cross-beam of the screen. Rood screens were revived in the later nineteenth century in many **Ecclesiological-movement** churches.

Saddleback tower: a tower with a gabled roof, sometimes intended as a temporary measure pending the building of a spire.

Sarcophagus: effectively a stone coffin, with a carved stone lid, and sometimes carved sides.

Scissor-beam roof: used to describe a roof in which the cross-ties are at an angle, intersecting each other in the middle in the manner of a saltire.

Scoto-catholic: a term used here to describe the Church of Scotland's version of the **Ecclesiological Movement,** which fell well short of the equivalent in the Scottish Episcopal Church in terms of recreating an imagined Mediaeval past.

Sedilia: the seats provided for assisting clergy in the chancel of a pre-Reformation church. Sedilia were canopied stone seats built into the south wall of the building.

Session house: a room provided for meetings of the Kirk Session, the governing body of a Presbyterian congregation, and of the civil parish of a Church of Scotland until the late nineteenth century. Sometimes session houses were detached buildings, or if attached to church buildings, were given distinct architectural expression.

Sounding board: the canopy above a pulpit, giving it dignity, but also reflecting the preacher's voice down and out to the congregation.

Stencilled decoration: made by cutting holes in waxed paper or cardboard and then forcing paint, by a stiff bristled brush, through the holes on to a flat or curved smooth surface. Stencilling was extensively used in Gothic Revival and Arts and Crafts churches to decorate walls, ceilings, beams and organ pipes. The rich effects in Gothic Revival churches have often been painted over, and partly reappear when the later paint peels off.

Tracery: the term used for the stonework within a window frame which divides up the glazed area, creating a pattern. See also **Curvilinear, Flamboyant, Geometric, Perpendicular** and **Plate.**

Transept: one of the side arms in a **cruciform** church.

Transitional: a term used to describe the period of transition from the **Romanesque** to early Gothic, in the late twelfth and early thirteenth century.

Trapezoidal: a term in geometry used to describe a four-sided shape with two sides parallel. One of the parallel sides is shorter than the other, so that the two other sides slope towards it. In churches the trapezoid is regular, so that the non-parallel sides slope in at the same angle.

Tympanum: the word used to describe the space within the head of an arch, especially a round-headed arch. In **Romanesque**

architecture this semicircular space is often filled with low-relief sculpture.

Vault: a roof made of stone to an arched profile. There are many ways of forming a vaulted roof, but essentially there are three possible principles: the **barrel vault,** the rib vault, and the **fan vault.** In the rib vault an interlocking system of cut stone forms a web, and rubble stones are used to fill the spaces in between. Occasionally the infilling stones are carefully cut to fit. In many churches the roof is of timber, and a plaster ceiling has been installed to resemble stone vaulting. In some late nineteenth and early twentieth-century churches the ceiling is of wooden strips in the form of vaulting.

Vernacular: here used to describe buildings or features which are similar in character to simpler secular buildings, and constructed in a similar manner. This is not a precise term, and its application is somewhat subjective.

Wagon roof: a term used to describe a timber roof where the tie beams are some way up the rafters. In many such roofs a plaster or timber ceiling has been formed under the structural members.

Index